There Are No Buts Except The One You Are Sitting On

Mark Tollefson

Copyright © 2013 Mark Tollefson

All rights reserved.

ISBN:0992031915

ISBN-13: 978-0992031916

All scripture quotations, unless otherwise indicated, are taken from the Holy Bible, New International Version®, NIV®. Copyright ©1973, 1978, 1984, 2011 by Biblica, Inc.™ Used by permission of Zondervan. All rights reserved worldwide. www.zondervan.com The "NIV" and "New International Version" are trademarks registered in the United States Patent and Trademark Office by Biblica, Inc.™

Cover Photography—Paula Tollefson

Editing—Ashley West

There Are No Buts Except The One You Are Sitting On

DEDICATION

This book is dedicated to my wife Liz whom God has used over the past 29 years to teach me about walking with Him and living the abundant life that He came to earth to provide for us to live.

Mark Tollefson

CONTENTS

Acknowledgments	i
Foreword	3
1-The Issue	8
2-Being a Disciple	28
3-Child of the King	51
4-Don't Worry	65
5-Defeating Worry	76
6-I Must Forgive	108
7-The Two Sides Of Forgiveness	125
8-The ME Generation	141
9-The Beginning	164

ACKNOWLEDGMENTS

Thanks to all those that supported and encouraged me as I worked on this project

Join us on Facebook
www.facebook.com/ThereAreNoButsExceptTheOneYouAreSittingOn

Foreword

In the Christmas season that just went by my wife, Liz, and I took our granddaughter, Kira out Christmas shopping. As any grandparents would we enjoyed our time with her thoroughly. There is something special about the Christmas season as seen through a child's eye. Kira was three years old at the time and I realized her understanding of what Christmas was really about was limited due to her age. Like any three year old, as she watched the commercials on television she would turn to me or whoever was with her at the time and inform us that she wanted us to buy that particular toy for her. My standard response was "we will see, maybe for Christmas". This response seemed to be satisfactory to her at that age.

I asked at one point who was born at Christmas and her response was that she was born at Christmas. As I reflected on that response I realized that it was somewhat appropriate for her mindset at the time. After all, Christmas seemed to be all about her, she got presents and both sets of her grandparents were eager to take her out shopping. So in her mind, it must be her birthday.

I had decided that as we went Christmas shopping I wanted to find some sort of medium to help Kira understand the real reason we take time to celebrate this holiday. I was looking for anything, a video, a book, or really anything that would help to teach her about the fact that we celebrate the birth of our Savior and Lord, Jesus. I must admit I knew I could have gone straight to the local Christian bookstore and it would have been easy to find something that would fit the bill perfectly. However, I decided that my quest, at the beginning, would be limited to the regular retail outlets one would go to during any shopping excursion.

This turned out to be an interesting and educational experience to say the least. As we traveled from store to store we would see the usual items you would expect to see at this time of year. We of course found Santa Claus, snowmen, reindeer, candy canes, and there was plenty of candy. There were countless Christmas videos, mostly from popular shows that all taught about what I would consider the secular meaning to the season. Most of the videos and books that were available would try to teach some lesson such as being kind to your fellow man, thinking of others at this season or even about being a good girl so Santa brings you presents. While all of these are good lessons to teach it still did not talk about the coming of our Savior. I finally relented and made a visit to our local Christian bookstore and while there; I found exactly what I had been searching for during my quest.

What I realized during this search was the fact that we do not live in a Christian country anymore. This of course is not a new revelation to most of you who are reading this book. It did, however, drive the fact home that we have secularized our culture to the point that our Christian roots have been lost in many areas. As I reflected on this fact, I was contemplating how we as Christians were to lift the name of Jesus up in a world that has become increasingly hostile toward the God of the Bible. How can we as Christians live in a way that would make people stand up and take notice of the Gospel?

When I look at the New Testament church I would wonder how the gospel spread so fast and how did they draw others to Jesus in a world that was not a lot different from ours today. As you look into the book of Acts you quickly discover that the secret was the life that they lived. They lived the life that Jesus intends all of us to live in the power of the Holy Spirit. When those around them saw the difference that Jesus made in their way of living they knew something had changed them. This is why I felt led to write this book. If we who are called by His name would live the victorious life that God intended, then even in our secularized society people may be able to argue about many things but they would not be able to deny the change that has been brought into our lives. As you read through this book, take time to examine yourself, and see where you fit into God's plan.

"The thief comes only to steal and kill and destroy; I have come that they may have life, and have it to the full" (John 10:10).

There Are No Buts Except The One You Are Sitting On

1

The Issue

"He replied, 'you of little faith, why are you so afraid?' Then he got up and rebuked the winds and the waves, and it was completely calm."

Matthew 8:26

Have you ever wondered why someone would buy a high performance car only to drive it on residential streets in the city? I heard about a car and it's a 2012 Cadillac CTS-V sedan. At the time of production it was said to be the world's fastest sedan. It came off the factory floor with a 6.2 litre supercharged engine and a whopping 556 horsepower. It has 551 foot pounds of torque and can do 0-60 in 3.9 seconds. The starting price was $64,515. How would you like to be behind the wheel of that powerhouse all done in a Cadillac body.

So you know the comfort would be incredible. Now imagine, owning one of these cars and driving it off the showroom floor only to spend the rest of the time driving it like it was a 1966 Volkswagen Beetle. Not only would you be wasting a fine automobile but people would look at you and wonder why you bought the car in the first place if you never used it for how it was intended.

Well then, my question for you and the purpose of this book is: Why do we follow and serve a God as great as we do, yet we live our lives as if we are serving some idol made of wood that really cannot do anything for us? It has been a concern of mine for some time that there are many Christians living defeated lives. They are not experiencing the victorious life that God has planned for us. I am not saying that when we are Christians and walk with God that we will not have troubles in life. In fact the exact opposite is the truth according to Jesus. But we can live this life in victory despite the difficulties.

The following passage from Matthew defines the Christian walk.

"Therefore everyone who hears these words of mine and puts them into practice is like a wise man who built his house on the rock. The rain came down, the streams rose, and the winds blew and beat against that house; yet it did not fall, because it had its foundation

on the rock. But everyone who hears these words of mine and does not put them into practice is like a foolish man who built his house on sand. The rain came down, the streams rose, and the winds blew and beat against that house, and it fell with a great crash." (Matthew 7: 24-27).

From this we can see that it is not a matter of if the rain comes but instead of just a matter of when it comes. This is what defines the difference among the man who built his life on the words of God, he survived, and was victorious; however, the one who took his eyes off Christ, his fall, was great. It is not a matter of will we go through tough times but a matter of how we go through those times.

It is a sad reality; Christians seem to be walking through this life in the same way and manner as the rest of the world. There are times when it seems there are no really discernible differences among the way the world approaches difficulties and the way the Christians deal with these same issues. Yes, we are good at taking a stand on some issues like abortion and same sex marriage; however, when we are faced with personal crises we deal with it with the same fear and apprehension as the non-Christians. What kind of example is this setting for the world? Why would non-

Christians want what we have, for when the crunch comes it appears we are all the same?

We need to define the use of Christian and non-Christian throughout this book. When discussing the definition of a Christian the only real source of truth would be the Bible, specifically defined in the book of Romans. This book gives us a run-down on our spiritual condition but offers a solution to the problem we are experiencing. In Romans 10, we see the simplest yet concise definition of what God says a Christian is and that is the definition referenced in this book.

"If you declare with your mouth, 'Jesus is Lord', and believe in your heart that God raised him from the dead, you will be saved. For it is with your heart that you believe and are justified, and it is with your mouth that you profess your faith and are saved" (Romans 10: 9-10).

One that confesses that Jesus is Lord will be submitted to his will and will be doing the will of God. As the passage states it is not just a verbal declaration but also a heart commitment. In other words, if you confess with your mouth, then you must live your life while serving God and doing His will. If you have not surrendered your life to God, and you are still serving-self and the devil then you would fall into the category of non-Christian. Unlike some people have asserted, there are only two groups of people in this world, some would like to suggest that there is a third group of people who are safe but that is just not biblical. Jesus states, **"Whoever is not with me is against me, and whoever does not gather with me scatters" (Matthew 12: 30).**

Romans 12:1-2, accurately show us the result of making Jesus Lord**, "Therefore, I urge you, brothers and sisters, in view of God's mercy, to offer your bodies as a living sacrifice, holy and pleasing to God—this is your true and proper worship. Do not conform to the pattern of this world but be transformed by the renewing of your mind. Then you will be able to test and approve what God's will is —his good, pleasing and perfect will. Then, we will be transformed and we will no longer walk according to the rules of this present world."** We line up our thinking with God's way of doing things and believe me that is the best way to operate in this world.

It is important for us to take time to define certain thoughts we are talking about. We should never assume in today's world that just because someone is using the same words and phrases that we are using that it automatically follows that they mean the same thing as we are intending.

I cannot help see the church today and have a heavy heart. I see professing Christians that are living lives that are not all that different from their neighbours, they go to work, and you cannot tell them from the world. They seem to be consumed by the same distractions that non- Christians are distracted with. They seem to be caught up in the same distractions that the non- Christians are taken up with. They seem to be pursuing all those things that moth and rust will destroy and they do not even realize this fact. They are worrying about the same things in which the world is consumed by and they do not seem to be offering many answers to a dying and hurting world even though God tells us, we should be the exact opposite. God expects us to show the world the way as it states in the following verse, **"But in your hearts revere Christ as Lord. Always be prepared to give an answer to everyone who asks you to give the reason for the hope that you have. But do this with gentleness and respect" (1 Peter, 3: 15).** Why would they ask any questions when they cannot see the hope in us? If hope is in us should it not be coming out of us like a sweet smell?

Have you ever walked by one of those places in the mall that bakes cinnamon buns? Does that smell not just make you want to stand around that area all day? Does it really make you want to buy some? What about that new car smell? Scents just come off things and those that it comes off may have little or no control over what scent they are giving off. Or it may be intentional; you cannot tell me it is an accident that all you can smell within 20 feet of those cinnamon places is that distinctive odour. That is what we need to be doing as Christians, we need to be giving off an odour that is unmistakable, and a smell that attracts others to the God we serve. It seems that sometimes we give off an odour that seems to repel people or that we do not give off an odour at all.

Have you ever dealt with something that had a very strong odour? I remember when we first moved to our farm we live on we had sheep. Sheep are fairly easy animals to tend to and there are many lessons that can be learned from caring for them but there is one thing that I remember specifically—it was the smell. It was not that it was a bad smell but what I remember is the fact that on those occasions when you had to work with them at close range, perhaps while giving them immunizations, was that the smell would stay with you for a few days even though they were not around. I could be driving in the car the next day and I would still be able to smell them. It was not that it was unpleasant or that I did not take a shower, it was just like the smell was imprinted on my brain. That is what we need to be as Christians. When we leave the room we need to leave our smell behind. We need to leave the imprint of Christ on their minds even when we are not around.

Have you ever had a teacher that just made a subject come alive for you? Maybe it was a subject that you were never really interested in before but after a couple classes with a certain teacher you were just drawn to the subject matter. At the time you may not have been able to put your finger on just what it was about that instructor but there was something there that just seemed to motivate you to dive deeper into that subject matter.

Well, I had one of those teachers. I can remember how that got me really interested in history. I was going to Polk Community College in Winter Haven, Florida and I had to take history for one of my credits. I found myself in an American history class with a teacher, that to be honest with you, I do not even remember his name. I can, however, see him in my mind. He was a short, grey haired, man with glasses, and to be frank was somewhat of a boring teacher. He was an accurate portrayal of someone who could be very old school and I am sure that many students could not wait to get out of his class.

I would, as in most of my classes sit in the back of the room trying to go unnoticed. As I listened to this man go through the course there was something about him that intrigued me. He was not just teaching history for a paycheck. He seemed to genuinely enjoy what he was doing, he actually enjoyed history. Imagine that, people actually enjoyed learning this stuff. As I look back I may not have actually realized it at that time but this was the defining moment which jump started my interest in history. If he found this so fascinating, than maybe there was something to history worth investigating. Maybe, I should take notice of what he had to say. As they say the rest is history.

The point to that story is simple. If we are living this Christian life the way God intended us to and we are victorious in our walk, then maybe more people would stand up, take notice, and want to know what we have, and what they clearly do not have. Do you often wonder why it is, that churches are not growing, or one big question is, why the younger generation leaves church in such high volume after they reach a certain age. Well, maybe if our children saw us living out a victorious and fruitful life instead of just going through the motions things might be different. They would realize there is more to following Jesus than just some rituals and traditions we follow on Sunday. They would see that when we follow the Lord our lives are different and when I say different I mean better.

There is another more selfish reason for wanting people to live up to their calling as Christians. It simply is a fantastic life to live. It is a life that is full of all the same things the rest of the world goes through. We have our ups and downs but we live in a victorious way. In John 10: 10, Jesus states, *"The thief comes only to steal and kill and destroy; I have come that they may have life and have it to the full."* Here he tells us in a very clear manner that the world's way, or Satan's way, is to destroy us. Why would we still want the world's way? Why is it that, although, we say we are following God we look at what the world is doing with envy? Why would we think we can mix the world's ways in with God's plan and somehow be more successful than if we just stuck with God's plan?

If we really look at it when we say we have the faith in God but we do not live a victorious life, do we really have much faith in Him at all? That kind of faith is the same type of faith a sports fan has in their team. They say they love their team but when things do not go the way they hope, all a sudden they feel they can do a better job managing the team then the person who is paid to do so. When their team plays a stronger team they root for their favourite team; inside they do not actually have the faith to believe that their team can be victorious. People refer to this as being realistic, especially when it comes to a sport; however, when it comes to God that kind of thinking is simply a lack of faith and knowledge of whom God really is and what He has planned for the world today.

So why are Christians living this defeated and broken life? Why are we not experiencing what God really has for us? In Hebrews 5:12, it states, ***"In fact, though by this time you ought to be teachers, you need someone to teach you the elementary truths of God's word all over again. You need milk, not solid food."***

Paul tells the Corinthian church the same thing, ***"Brothers and sisters, I could not address you as people who live by the Spirit but as people who are still worldly —mere infants in Christ. I gave you milk, not solid food, for you were not yet ready for it. Indeed, you are still not ready. You are still worldly. For since there is jealousy and quarreling among you, are you not worldly? Are you not acting like mere humans?" (1 Corinthians 3: 1-3)***

Here we have Paul addressing an established church, one that was having the same problems we have today. This was a church that should have known better. They had already received the fundamentals and should have progressed beyond but were still acting like the rest of the world.

There was no difference among them and their neighbours. The church at Corinth was experiencing many problems; there were divisions and people were following different people. In 1 Corinthians 1: 12, he tells them what he means by this division. ***"What I***

mean is this: One of you says, 'I follow Paul'; another, 'I follow Apollos'; another, 'I follow Cephas'; still another, 'I follow Christ'." Does this sound familiar? How many people today will follow one pastor or another, instead of quoting the Bible, they quote an author? There are many people who will go to a particular church, not to hear from God but only because a particular pastor is there.

There was sexual immorality in the church; in fact it was of the sort that Paul says is not even named among the gentiles. Could he have hit them any harder than with a comment like that? They were going to the courts to sue one another, asking those that did not know Christ to mediate among Christian brothers. Paul even asks if they have people wise enough to mediate such disputes without going to the world for their answers. There were marriage problems, food problems, problems of keeping order in the church, and apparently there was confusion concerning spiritual gifts. The problems with spiritual gifts lead to a problem of pride. There were problems with their theology and the fact that false doctrines had crept into the church. Does any of this sound familiar?

There are times when we look at people of the previous centuries and we feel we would have acted differently in the same situation. Looking around I believe we would have acted no differently. That fact is proved by the fact that after all these years and having their example to follow we seem to be still falling into the same problems and traps of Satan that they were getting caught up in.

So what was the basis of the problem with the Corinthian church? All the issues that Paul referenced were really symptoms of the actual illness. Often we concentrate on the symptoms forgoing the origin of the disease.

Imagine if you were hurt in a car accident and they had you taken to the best hospital in the country, given the best doctor, and only treated for the pain. How well do you think you would do in the long term? If the doctor did not actually treat the injury that was the root of the pain, you may be a little more comfortable while the pain was being managed; however, you would never experience the healing your body requires.

I can remember several years ago, I was injured badly in an accident at work. I had a couple of my fingers crushed under a large and heavy load. When they got me to the hospital the first thing they did was to administer morphine to me. The morphine they gave to me did two things: first, it made me nauseous; secondly, it helped manage the intense pain. The interesting thing about it was the fact that, although, I could still feel some pain it had subsided to a manageable level. In fact

I can say that I really was not too concerned overall about the little pain I was still in at that moment. However, it was not until the doctor tended to my wounds and I had the therapy I needed as a result of the injury that the real healing had begun. The medication merely helped mask the problem. This is what we are doing in the church today; we are comforting people, and covering up the problem. We do not seem to be challenging people to go deeper into their faith walk.

This is exactly what Paul had to deal with in the Corinthian church and what we have to deal with in today's church. As we read through 1 Corinthians, we see the problem with that church was that they were relying on the world's wisdom to solve and deal with the normal issues that come up in life. It was not that they had problems that were unique to them, but instead of looking to God for his way and the only way to deal with their everyday walk, they thought it would be a good idea to a take some of God's wisdom, and mix the world's wisdom as well, and expecting everything would work out. They could not have been more wrong. It is like trying to mix oil and water; they just do not go together. If you put antifreeze in the engine oil of a car, the car will run for a while but at some point the bearings will be ruined, the motor will seize up, and then you will go nowhere until the problem is dealt with. It may not happen immediately but be sure it will happen.

The Corinthian church had the Old Testament prophets to read, and they had the apostles to teach them. It is possible that some in that church had actually seen Christ when he was on earth. Today, we have the Bible to read, and we have the history to look back on to help teach us the way we should be living for God. We live in a time where we have access to more information than any other time in history but we still seem to get it wrong when it comes to our spiritual life and our walk with God. We have access to many commentaries, radio programs, TV programs, Bible studies, and numerous translations of the Bible at our fingertips. In fact, we can have all that information on a smart-phone that fits into our pocket. You would think that with all that we would rarely get it wrong, how unfortunate it is that at times, we seem to be no better than the first century Corinthian church.

So, the question is, if we have access to all the things we have and we can see what the New Testament churches had access to, what they did including the apostles why are we still living like we do? Why are we still having the same struggles they did and the same struggles we have seen people have for years. We see some people dealing with the same issues and they seem to stay at the same spiritual level as they were at the day they were saved. They never seem to progress to the victorious life that God wants them to have.

I am sure that much of the New Testament Christians understood what it meant to be saved. Just like today, plenty of Christians know what is in the Bible, and how they may even understand much of what has been transcribed for us by God; however, like the Christians of Paul's time we are allowing the world's thinking to come into the church. We think that although God's Word is true we somehow seem to think that we need to mix the world's wisdom in with it, so that it can make sense to our minds. It is amazing to me that there are times when I will be going over a Biblical principle with people and I will hear the following:

- "Well I know that is true…but."

- "I know the Bible says we are not supposed to worry…but."

- "I really want to leave all my burdens with God…but."

- "I know we serve a big God, and nothing is impossible with Him…but."

They will always have a reason they cannot or should not just believe what the Bible tells them. Sometimes,

Christians just do not know what the Bible tells us and do not understand who God really is. Other times, Christians have mixed the world's way of doing things with God's way. This is a combination destined for failure.

As the title of this book suggests when it comes to putting the principles of God as outlined in the Bible into practice there are simply no buts. There is one time when the use of the word BUT would be appropriate and that is when we are using it in the context, "...but God." In other words, you may say something such as, "I used to have trouble with worry but with God I do not worry anymore." When the word but is followed by the word God then everything is changed in the direction that it was intended to be before the beginning of time. When we use the word but to say that we cannot follow the principles that God laid out in His Word, then we are really saying that God does not know what He is talking about. We are simply making excuses for our poor behaviour or an excuse to stay where we are in our walk with Him. These excuses are simply not good enough, they will not change the word of God, nor will they change what he expects of us.

My purpose in writing this book is to try to encourage Christians to live life the way God intended us to live. My desire is that we, through God's word, live a victorious Christian walk. A walk that would make those around us stand up, take notice, wanting to know why we have hope in the midst of turmoil, and why we are not broken like the rest of the world when the times get tough.

In the next chapters I will look at some of the common ways that we really miss what God has for us. We will look at the areas of life where we are not really living the kind of abundant life that Jesus said He came to give us. I will not just list off ways we are lacking, I will also offer some ways that we can get back on track in our Christian walk. I believe we need to offer practical ways to put the principles of God to work in our lives. When we get it right and start living like God intended us to live, we will find out just how satisfying this life with Christ can be. It is not that our lives will be without challenges, but we can, through the power of the Holy Spirit, rise above those challenges and be an example to the world around us and our families.

So, sit back and be ready to be challenged. Be ready to be radical for Christ. Be ready to look at life and its problems the way God does. Be ready to live a life that is so exciting you will never get enough of it, and you will want to go deeper. When you live life the way God intended there will be no turning back and you will wonder how you could have lived to this point, while just drinking milk.

Questions for Reflection

1. Are you experiencing the abundant life that God has called you to and do those around see a hope in you?

2. What areas of your walk with God are you rationalizing so that you do not have to follow the way God wants you to live?

There Are No Buts Except The One You Are Sitting On

2

Being a Disciple

"Then he said to them all: 'Whoever wants to be my disciple must deny themselves and take up their cross daily and follow me'. "

Luke 9:23

What does it mean to be a disciple of Christ? When you think of the word disciple what comes to your mind? In the church in North America, we have sold an easy type of discipleship, we have sold it as being a free gift, and there is nothing we need to do. I need to mention that the Bible is clear, that the gift of salvation is free, and that there is nothing we can do to earn salvation. The only way we can reconcile with God, is through the atoning work of Christ on the cross, and His bodily resurrection. There were times in the New Testament that Jewish believers would fall back and try to do something to earn their salvation. I am not suggesting that we can, or that we have to, earn this great salvation that God has given us. But the question is, once we have accepted that gift of grace that God offers to us, what does it look like to live our lives as His disciples? The Bible has a lot to say about the life of a disciple, and I want to take this chapter to look briefly at what it is like to be a true disciple of Christ.

The first question that comes to mind is the following, if salvation is a free gift does it cost us anything? I know that on the surface this question seems like a contradiction itself but as we look into the biblical definition of a true disciple of Christ, we see that the answer is plain. Not only does it cost us something but it indeed costs us everything. It requires we give up our life and our own control, to give total control of our future, and our present to God Himself. ***"Whoever finds their life will lose it, and whoever loses their life for my sake will find it." (Matthew 10: 39)*** The thought, if I accept this free gift and follow God, while I continue to call all the shots is simply wrong. It is the world's view of God, thinking they can just add God to a list of beliefs which they already have; this thinking is not supported anywhere in scripture.

We sometimes act like it is just another accessory we acquire. In fact, when we look into the gospels we see very a different idea. The following passage is from the Gospel of Luke, and it comes as people ask about following Him. You would think in times like this Jesus would be encouraging them to follow but, Jesus, does not react as we or His disciples expect Him to; whereas, we would minimize the negative aspects and build up the positive ones, Jesus seems almost to discourage them.

"As they were walking along the road, a man said to him, 'I will follow you wherever you go.' Jesus replied, 'Foxes have dens and birds have nests, but the Son of Man has no place to lay his head.' He said to another man, 'Follow me'. But he replied, 'Lord, first let me go and bury my father.' Jesus said to him, 'Let the dead bury their own dead, but you go and proclaim the kingdom of God.' Still another said, 'I will follow you, Lord; but first let me go back and say goodbye to my family.' Jesus replied, 'No one who puts a hand to the plow and looks back is fit for service in the kingdom of God'" (Luke 9: 57-62).

Does this sound like a faith that cost nothing and is easy? I would say not. Jesus lays it on the line for them and tells them that it will cost them everything to follow Him. I would say that when Jesus said this to us it meant that we needed to be all in, there was no half way with Christ, and it was an all or nothing life. This is again borne out in Matthew 12: 30, **"Whoever is not with me is against me, and whoever does not gather with me scatters."** This is not the picture of someone who is just in on Sunday. It, however, is not the type of discipleship we seem to sell to people today. It is though, what Jesus taught about being a disciple.

I believe it is necessary to point out here that being all in does not mean that you suddenly have it all together and you will never make a mistake again. I am not saying that at the moment of conversion you suddenly become someone who has it all together and you understand everything there is to know about God. Being all in is more of a mindset than it is an action, although, it will translate into your actions. It does mean that every part of you and your life belongs to God, and you hold nothing back from God. This is a heart issue, which means that if your heart is all in, than Jesus can work with you. He will show you areas of your life that need work and the Holy Spirit will work with you on those areas to bring them under God's dominion. I wonder if we cling to the notion that we can be Christian without being all in because it defends our mediocre Christian walk. Does it make us more comfortable to think that if everyone else is in the same boat then I am okay?

To see how the concept of total commitment as a disciple started we need to go back to the Old Testament. The idea of being completely sold out to God is not a new concept. If we look at the law we see how it affected every aspect of a person's life. The Old Testament law contained 613 rules to be followed. As you go through the Old Testament law we see how it covers every aspect of life. It was not just about the church life of the Israelite, it was about their entire life. It was expected that their all areas of their lives would bring glory to God, by doing so they would show the other nations who God was, and what he is about. It took the Israelites following all these laws before God promised them great blessing. God did not tell them to follow the ones they liked and He would bless them, He instructed them, it was all or nothing. We see this from the following passage in Joshua.

"Be strong and very courageous. Be careful to obey all the law my servant Moses gave you; do not turn from it to the right or to the left, that you may be successful wherever you go. Do not let this Book of the Law depart from your mouth; meditate on it day and night, so that you may be careful to do everything written in

it. Then you will be prosperous and successful" (Joshua 1: 7-8).

Let us start off our look at the Old Testament by looking at the Ten Commandments as they are found in Exodus 20. God spoke all these words:

"'I am the Lord your God, who brought you out of Egypt, out of the land of slavery You shall have no other gods before me.

You shall not make for yourself an idol in the form of anything in heaven above or on the earth beneath or in the waters below. You shall not bow down to them or worship them; for I, the Lord your God, am a jealous God, punishing the children for the sin of the fathers to the third and fourth generation of those who hate me, but showing love to a thousand generations of those who love me and keep my commandments.

You shall not misuse the name of the Lord your God, for the Lord will not hold anyone guiltless who misuses his name.

Remember the Sabbath day by keeping it holy. Six days you shall labour and do all your work, but the seventh day is a Sabbath to the Lord your God. On it you shall not do any work, neither you, nor your son or daughter, nor your manservant or maidservant, nor your animals, nor the alien within your gates. For in six days the Lord made the heavens and the earth, the sea, and all that is in them, but he rested on the seventh day. Therefore the Lord blessed the Sabbath day and made it holy.

Honor your father and your mother, so that you may live long in the land the Lord your God is giving you.

You shall not murder.

You shall not commit adultery

You shall not steal.

You shall not give false testimony against your neighbour.

You shall not covet your neighbour's house. You shall not covet your neighbour's wife, or his manservant or maidservant, his ox or donkey, or anything that belongs to your his manservant or maidservant, his ox or donkey, or anything that belongs to your neighbour'" (Exodus 20: 1-17).

If we start with the first four commandments we will quickly see how they cover what we consider the spiritual part of our lives. When God tells them that they shall have no other Gods before Him, He is covering a large area. Unfortunately, we look at this and simply see it as a command that only involves our spiritual side of life, and we sometimes fail to see that it alone seeps into every area of life. We will confine these commandments to our church life and fail to see that what we worship and how we worship will involve our whole life. I just want you to think for a moment about the job you have currently. Take a few minutes in which to contemplate how much your job affects every aspect of your life. It dictates when you eat lunch, what time you get up, how you get there, when you take vacation, when you sleep, and even how much time you spend with your family. Did you ever think your employer controlled that much of your life? You probably thought you were in control. Whether you are the CEO of a company or the brand new employee on the block working your way up, the company you work for will have this much control over your life and if it does not then most likely you will be looking for another place to work.

If a company you work for has this much control over you then imagine to what degree who or what you worship will affect your life. Whatever you worship will affect all aspects of your life, it will completely control you and your behaviour. When God told us not to serve any other Gods the word serve was an excellent choice of words. That is clearly what we do when we worship anything. The thing we worship has complete control over us. We can worship many things, family, money, celebrities, other gods, friends, and even pleasure to name but a few. So the question becomes who or what do you want to control your behaviour? Do you want the things of this world that we know will pass away to rule over the way you live your life or do you want the God of Creation that is passionate about you to take control. When you compare the eternal God to another thing that we may find important, all those other things will pale in comparison to giving our lives over in worship to Him.

As if the first four commandments do not give us enough, God gives His people six more that will reach into every area of their lives. The next six commandments get even more specific when it comes to our day to day life with each other. They cover our family relationships and our relationships with everyone else. They cover our moral values and our relationship with our spouse. The commandments tell us how we are to deal with others, possessions, how we are to be honest, and even deal with our thought process when it comes to coveting. When God gives them the commandment about coveting, He even is specific on what they are not to covet. Then just if you thought you might be able to slip one by, He finishes by telling us not to covet anything of our neighbours; I guess we can say that really covers it all.

For our next step in the journey let us take a quick walk through the book of Leviticus. This book is full of statutes that God gave to His people, through His servant Moses. If we go to the end of the book, it states, **"These are the commands the Lord gave Moses on Mount Sinai for the Israelites" (Leviticus 27: 34).** Now let us break down the book a little, to get a better grasp, on what God expected from his people and as we do this remember, again, that being a disciple is an all in process, we can hold nothing back from God.

The book starts off with seven chapters about the various sacrifices that God required. These chapters are very specific on what acceptable sacrifices were and how they were to be conducted. There was a prescribed way that they were to be offered and God demanded that they be done the way He told them. There were five separate sacrifices and each had a purpose. Then in Chapter Eight, we have Aaron and his sons being consecrated for service as the priests, and in the next chapter their priestly service begins. The next chapter gives us a story about a profane fire from the sons of Aaron and the results of that and then we are told how the priest is to act.

The next ten chapters are spent giving the people many rules to cover all aspects of life. God tells them how to handle everything from dietary laws to moral statues, how to handle lepers, even to laws about bodily discharges. Are you getting the point yet? The next few chapters go over more rules for the priests, they establish which feasts are to be celebrated and even how to care for some articles of the temple. In Chapter 25, it deals with how to handle the land and even how to lend to the poor.

Chapter 26 brings us to God announcing blessings, and penalties for obeying, as well as, disobeying the law. As you read through this chapter, there is something very interesting we will see about God. I have to say it is not something we expect to see from the God of the Old Testament. We need to remember that God is the same, yesterday, today, and forever, so it is really not a surprise when we see God's grace at work in the book of Leviticus. We see in this chapter that God tells them if they keep His statutes, then He will bless them and give them what they need to live an abundant life. If they disobey the statutes, He will punish them; however, as we read through the various punishments that God will pronounce on them it is a gradual process. He does not just write them off at the first problem but He takes them through a system of progressive discipline, and each time they ignore His commands it gets worse. The whole purpose of these punishments is to bring His people back to Himself. It is about reconciliation. The final chapter covers redeeming persons and property dedicated to the Lord.

I hope this quick trip through Leviticus will show you how God is not just interested in being part of your life but instead wants to be part of every aspect of your life. We can say that He wants your entire life that is how much He loves you. Next time you read through a book such as Leviticus, do not just skip over it because you think it is a book for other people and another time. Read it with the thought in mind that God is interested in every aspect of our lives and He wants the best for us. Look at it with the knowledge that God cares so much about His people; He took the time to give them laws which covered every area of their lives so that He could show other nations what they could experience by worshiping Him.

Let us move back into the New Testament and look at what is called, the Sermon on the Mount, found in Matthew 5-7. When we are talking about what a disciple is this is a great passage and it paints a clear picture of how we should be acting if we are truly His disciples. Many people will look to this section and try to find a bunch rules to follow. God, on the other hand, meant this for so much more. Jesus here was introducing a whole new way of living. A way that was not simply a bunch of rules to follow, but instead a life where He will write his commandments on our hearts and will make us new creations so we can live this life and not only just live it but we will desire to live this way.

Right off in chapter 5, Jesus hits us with what I will call the 'Six Principles of Living'. He starts each one off with the phrase, "you have heard", and then proceeds to tell a new way to look at each situation. It is a way that He will change us with His Spirit to the point that not only will we not do these things but we will not want to go against the way He desires us to live. He picks six areas that cover every aspect of our lives here on earth.

The first area Jesus talks about starting in verse 21 is murder. Now, you may think this does not apply to me because I have never murdered anyone, and I never expect that I will be doing it either. This is where Jesus makes it interesting and He tells them that not only should you not murder but you should not even be mad at your brother without cause. He then tells us to agree to our adversary quickly. This is the first area Jesus addresses and it is all about our relationships with other people—even those we do not get along with too well. This section can be applied to all our earthly relationships.

Next, Jesus moves from murder to adultery. Would you put those two thoughts together if you were doing the talking? He takes it further than just committing adultery to simply engaging in the thought of adultery. With the Spirit it is now just not a matter of what we do but it is now about our heart attitude. So, we have covered our relationships with people and now He addresses our sexual attitudes and thoughts.

In verse 31, He moves into the marriage relationship. He here again shows the people who with the Spirit there is much more expected of them. Jesus looks at our commitment to our spouse and marriage. This deals with the core relationship of our lives. How we view our marriage relationship will come out in many ways in our walk with God.

In Verse 33, Jesus, starts teaching us about taking oaths. Some misinterpret this passage but as we look at it we get a clear picture of what He is saying. He is simply telling us that we should be living in such a way which people do not even need us to take an oath. This is because they will see the way we live our lives and they will be assured that when we say something that it will be the truth. This comes into play in every area of our lives. If people see that we cannot be trusted in one area, then they will certainly not trust us when we make a statement. We simply cannot live some areas of our life in one way, but are unreliable in others, and expect people to trust us, and that is why we need to be consistent in every area of our life. That is why we need to be all in as Disciples of Christ. When some areas of our lives are not under His control, the world will see us, and will tell us that we are hypocritical. Do not think for a minute that your non-Christian friends are not watching you and how you respond in every situation.

In this next section, Jesus, addresses how we react when people ask us to help them. He starts off by telling us how to react to those that will do us harm. We are simply to turn the other cheek; we are not to seek revenge on those that harm us. Later in chapter 6, Jesus, tells us that we must forgive those that wrong us or He will not forgive us. We will revisit this in a later chapter.

 He goes on to tell us that if one asks us to go a mile then we are to go that extra mile with them. It is not good enough simply to do your minimum but instead you must do all you can. . This came when Roman soldiers were able to order you to carry their pack for a mile; however, were not entitled to have you carry it further. As we continue here you must remember that there was no love lost between the Romans and the people of Israel. You can imagine what the soldier's reaction might have been when you had gone the required distance and you offered to go further. He would most certainly wonder why you were willing to do that for him, which may have given you the opportunity to tell him why, and share God's love with him. The soldier did not have to wait to ask you when it was convenient for you to do that for him. Even when it is inconvenient for us we need to be ready to go above and beyond what is expected of us. What a great example it is when we do services for others in Jesus' name, even when it is in convenient for us. What an opportunity to draw others to Christ!

The last section we will look at here begins in verse 43. Here He looks at our relationship with our enemies. As I write this it even sounds odd that we would have, let alone think about our relationship with our enemies. This is precisely what being a disciple is about. Jesus is telling us that, although, we tend to write off those that do us harm, we may stop talking to them, block them on Facebook, or pretend we do not see them when we are in public, He is saying that how we treat these people, is what shows the world who we are following. It encompasses areas of our lives that we sometimes take for granted and seldom think about and yet God wants control over those areas of our lives. Imagine telling someone who is not a disciple to love their enemies, they would think you are crazy. When you go ahead a few years we see Jesus himself washing the feet of the disciple that would in a short time betray Him. We will continue this topic further in the book, in a chapter on forgiveness.

I think we can safely say that Jesus covered every area of our lives in this one encounter on a mountain. We can now turn to Colossians to see what Paul says about living for Christ, **"And whatsoever ye do in word or deed, do all in the name of the Lord Jesus, giving thanks to God and the Father by him" (Col. 3:17)**. I would say that Paul did not leave much room open for us to do anything for ourselves or for us to do anything our way. He is certainly talking about an all or nothing attitude. He tells us we need to do it all for God, it has nothing to do with us, it is all about God. Do you still think that God just wants to be an add-on in your life? This has been a crash course in what it means to be a disciple and books have been written on this subject and here is where we get to the usual comment. I know this is true but how do we get to this point of surrender?

The first place to start in any correction we need to make in our walk with God is to remember who the God we serve is and what He is like. We will discuss more about this in the chapter on worry; however, at this point I think we need to look no further than the first chapter of Colossians. Look at the following passage and just meditate on it for a few minutes before you read on. Let it really get into your heart.

"And we pray this in order that you may live a life worthy of the Lord and may please him in every way: bearing fruit in every good work, growing in the knowledge of God, being strengthened with all power according to his glorious might so that you may have great endurance and patience, and joyfully giving thanks to the Father, who has qualified you to share in the inheritance of the saints in the kingdom of light. For he has rescued us from the dominion of darkness and brought us into the kingdom of the Son he loves, in whom we have redemption, the forgiveness of sins. He is the image of the invisible God, the firstborn over all creation. For by him all things were created: things in heaven and on earth, visible and invisible, whether thrones or powers or rulers or authorities; all things were created by him and for him. He is before all things, and in him all things hold together. And he is the head of the body, the church; he is the beginning and the firstborn from among the dead, so that in everything he might have the supremacy. For God was pleased to have all his fullness dwell in him, and through him to reconcile to himself all things, whether things on earth or things in heaven, by making peace through his blood, shed on the cross. Once you were alienated from God and were enemies in your minds because of your evil behaviour. But now he has reconciled you by Christ's physical body through death

to present you holy in his sight, without blemish and free from accusation" (Colossians 1:10-22).

I really must ask how a person cannot give up everything to a God such as this. Why would we even think that our plans, our thoughts, our ideas are even close to what He has in mind? Why would we think that we cannot trust Him with absolutely every area of our lives? If you are reading these questions and you still think you need to hold something back from God, please I implore you, read the passage one more time. Take some time, do an in depth study on God, and see how your view of Him will change.

Another exercise a person needs to do is to take a look at the damage sin has done, to both us, and to this world. We need to look at a few verses that talk about this subject. In order to look at this we need to go no further than Genesis 3,

"So the Lord God said to the serpent, 'Because you have done this, cursed are you above all the livestock and all the wild animals! You will crawl on your belly and you will eat dust all he days of your life. And I will put enmity between you and the woman, and between your offspring and hers; he will crush your head, and you will strike his heel.' To the woman he said, 'I will greatly increase your pains in childbearing; with pain you will give birth to children. Your desire will be for

your husband, and he will rule over you.' To Adam he said, 'Because you listened to your wife and ate from the tree about which I commanded you, 'You must not eat of it,' cursed is the ground because of you; through painful toil you will eat of it all the days of your life. It will produce thorns and thistles for you and you will eat the plants of the field. By the sweat of your brow you will eat your food until you return to the ground, since from it you were taken, for dust you are and to dust you will return'" (Genesis 3:14-19).

We can see from the above passage what sin has done to this world. When we look at the pronouncements of God, we can see that sin has not only damaged our relationship with God but it has affected everything we interact with on this earth. We often refer to the facts that sin has brought death into the world but that is as far as we go. We really need to see that it has done damage to everything, including the earth. Can you imagine planting a garden and never having to worry about weeding the plants? Can you imagine interacting with the animal kingdom and not being concerned that they may attack us?

So, the obvious question here is what is the point of this when it comes to discipleship? What does this have to do with being all in and giving God everything? Well, first I am not suggesting that because the world has been completely affected by sin that by following God somehow we will escape the problems that sin has brought into the world. The Bible is clear that this is not the case. In Matthew 7, Jesus tells us about two houses, one built on the sand and the other on the rock. The one built on the rock is an analogy of us living our lives on the things of God. You will notice in this story that Jesus tells us that the storms came to both houses, the difference was that the one that was built on the rock was able to withstand the storms. When we have sold out to God, we will be able to go through, whatever comes our way.

We also need to look at the fact that since sin has had a negative impact on everything around us; the question would be why would we want to live our lives serving sin in any way? It seems, to be logical, that if you know something that is negative a person would want to stay away from that. If you see a burning house you would not think that it would be a place you would want to run into and go inside. You would not stand there and think that this would be a good time to go over for coffee. On the contrary you would stay away from the house and let the fire department resolve the fire. So, why would we want to run and join our lives with sin? We read in the Bible that the result of sin is spiritual death, yet some people still think it is okay to have a bit of sin in their lives. They think that they can have some part of

God and some part of the world. Why would we want to have any part of something that ultimately will bring death? The only one that we can securely give every aspect of our life to is Jesus. We can be "all in" with Jesus and hold nothing back and have a peace only He can give.

Questions for Reflection

1. As you honestly examine your life are there areas that you have not given to God?

2. Have you kept anything for yourself?

3. Why do we sometimes find it hard to completely surrender to Jesus?

4. How do the areas you are holding back affect your relationship with God?

Mark Tollefson

3

Child of the King

"Yet to all who did receive him, to those who believed in his name, he gave the right to become children of God."

John 1:12

Have you ever met anyone that did not think they could accomplish anything in life? If you talk to those people you will realize the reason they feel this way is because of whom they think they are and what others have told them about their worth. When you tell your children that they are capable of achieving great things they will begin to believe that it is actually true. If you tell them they are no good and never will amount to anything they will, after a while begin to believe that, and will live up to the lack of expectations that have been placed on them. We as Christian are also susceptible to this same disease. We need to realize who we really are in Christ, then we can, and will live up to the potential that we have as God's people. In today's world we are told that every belief is valid and that there is no real difference among any of them. This is a lie straight from Satan. When we as Christians fall for this line of worldly thinking and we make it part of our faith we will suffer because this belief. When we start to believe our faith is not much different with any other we will act in a way that demonstrates that lie.

I have seen many bumper stickers on vehicles that read, "I'm not perfect just forgiven." These stickers drive me crazy. Is that really what our faith amounts to, "I am just forgiven?" Imagine what we are saying about the sacrifice Jesus gave on the cross when we say; I am just forgiven, with such a cavalier attitude. Is that really all you think about what Jesus did for you?

Although, I do understand that being forgiven is an incredible blessing, there is so much more to this relationship that we have with God because of His love for His creation. We are minimizing the work of Jesus when we believe that this is all there is for us and we will live down to that expectation. May the Lord, forgive us for such an attitude.

Many times I have heard Christians refer to themselves in the following way, "I am just a sinner saved by grace." I have heard it from the pulpit, I have seen it in books, and I have heard it from Christian musicians and from people in my church. Although, I do understand the concept, and at times I understand what they are trying to say, it is still an incorrect view of us. It is not how God sees us and that is the most important person to be concerned about. We are not some miserable creature that is barely going to make it to heaven; we have been redeemed by the creator of the universe. We will look into what it really means to be redeemed in this chapter. As I sit here writing about the fact that we are redeemed, I get very excited.

Some Christians seem to take great joy in referring to themselves as sinners saved by grace. I believe there are a few reasons, why they do this; however, there are two big problems with using this term when referring to whom we are now in Christ. The first reason that Christians use this term is because they think that it makes them seem to be very humble. They think that if they embrace who they really are in Christ it will lead to pride. I must say currently that I do understand that we were sinners, saved by grace and as the Bible tells us that it was a gift, and it was not because of what we have done, but because of the sacrifice of Christ. We must not continue to identify ourselves in that manner because when we are saved we are given the righteousness of Jesus, we are a new creation, and we have the Holy Spirit living in us. We are again minimizing the work of the Christ and the fact that His death, burial, and resurrection has taken us from miserable sinners to children of the King. Another reason they like to use this phrase is because when they do fall, and do things they know they should not, it gives them an excuse for their behaviour. Since they are only sinners saved by grace, it would stand to reason that they would sin now and again. This is where the 'but' comes into play. "I know I should not do that but I am just a sinner saved by grace, so I am going to fall once in a while." "I know I am not supposed to sin but I am only human." When we have a wrong view of who we are it is easy to live up to our distorted view. Satan enjoys it when we think less of ourselves than we should; he loves it when we do not realize who we really are in Jesus.

Many people will use Romans 7, to support their argument that we are wretched creatures. They will turn to verse 13 to the end of the chapter where Paul is telling us about the fact that the things he wants to do, he does not do, and the things he does not want to do he does. They will use this to explain the Christian life, and when it comes to verse 24 and Paul refers to himself as a wretched man, they stop and take their identity from that point. The problem with that interpretation is that it is not the correct one. When we are doing an exegesis on a portion of scripture, we need to be very careful not to just take out of it what suits us, and fits our way of thinking. We always need to take the context into consideration as well. The historic, the cultural, and the Biblical context all need to be considered. When we do this with this passage we see that Paul does not intend us to leave with the idea that we are wretched creatures.

Chapter 7 is telling us about life under the law, and how the law cannot save from sin but it actually shows us our sin. He then goes on to talk about the battle he had, while under the law, and how he felt when fighting sin while under the law. When you look at verse 24, he is describing the state of one under the law as he moves to the next verse, and indeed the next chapter he tells us that now under Christ there is no longer any condemnation for those in Christ Jesus. In Chapter 8 verse 2, Paul tells us that through Jesus, we have been freed from the law of sin and death. The next part of the chapter talks about how we can live this life for God because of Christ. Paul tells us, when we are in the flesh we cannot please God, but then he tells us we are not in the flesh. This section of scripture should never be used to show that we are somehow these pathetic creatures, when we are Christians. The wretched man Paul describes is the one without Jesus.

The fact is that if you do a search in the New International Version (NIV) Bible you will find the word sinner or sinners is used a total of 63 times. Never, is the word used to describe one that is following God or shall we say a disciple. The word is always used to describe someone who is not following God at all. It is always used in a negative way. ***"For just as through the disobedience of the one man the many were made sinners, so also through the obedience of the one man the many will be made righteous" (Romans 5:19).*** This is just one of those examples of how the title of sinner is used in scripture. This particular verse shows us the clear distinction among a sinner and a child of God. As you can clearly see in this verse, and if you look at its context, Adam's sin made us sinners but Jesus' obedience made us righteous. A few verses previous to this one, in Romans 5:8, Paul tells us that God loved us so much that while we were still sinners Christ died for us. These scriptures are certainly not telling us that Jesus died for us when we were still sinners, and then He left us in that state, but it is telling us that we are now saved from sin. The book of Romans shows us who we were without Christ and it paints a very different picture of who we are with Christ. I want you to take some time to look up the word sinner or sinners in the Bible, and go through the definition of them, and you will see that as I have said, it is never used when talking about a true follower of Jesus.

The question now is who are we in Christ? The first concept I want to look at is that of being redeemed. The Bible talks a lot about being redeemed, I believe we tend to gloss over this term, and take it for granted at times. There have been several shows on TV lately about pawn shops around America. If you are familiar with the concept of pawn shops it will help you to have a better picture of what it means to be redeemed.

The basic concept of a pawnbroker is that if you are in need of money, and you have something of value, than you could take that item to a pawn shop. There the shop would give you part of the value of that item as a loan and then they would keep the item as security. You would have a specific amount of time to return to the shop and redeem your item. You would then do this by paying the original money owed plus a set amount of interest on top. If you did not have the money to redeem the item, or you did not want it back because you felt it was not of enough value for you to redeem, the pawn shop would then have the right to take possession of what it was you brought in, and sell it to someone else, because they now owned it.

In our world, today, we tend to think the concept of redemption as something new, when Jesus redeemed us, but that is not the case. When we look through the Old Testament, this concept of redemption was throughout the law and the history of the Israelites. Numbers 25 talks about the redemption of property; Numbers 27, talks about the redemption of people and property dedicated to God. In Deuteronomy 7:8, it talks about how God redeemed the people of Israel from slavery in Egypt. **But it was because the Lord loved you and kept the oath he swore to your ancestors that he brought you out with a mighty hand and redeemed you from the land of slavery, from the power of Pharaoh King of Egypt**. The redemption from slavery is a concept that is echoed throughout the book of Romans. Again the concept of redemption is the fact that someone pays or does something to release someone or something else from a pledge or debt. When we look at the fact that we have been redeemed by Jesus, we need really to understand the fact that before we were set free, we were slaves to sin. It was not that we had woke up one morning and decided to sin but we born to sin.

A good comparison to our condition when we are born is to that of the Israelites in Egypt. The Israelites had been in Egypt for 400 years, we need to realize that the people who were alive when God redeemed them, and brought them out of Egypt were born into slavery. They had known nothing but slavery; I am sure some just accepted that this was their way in life. I am sure some never dreamed that they would ever be free from their Egyptian task masters. That is when God stepped in and broke the chains of slavery.

In the same way we were born into sin; there was no option for us. We inherited our sinful nature from Adam and the fall. I have talked to people who believe there is no other way that they can live their lives apart from sin and they feel trapped. They do not realize or accept that there is another way of living their lives. This is the one place that the use of the word but is very appropriate, we were without hope and we could never redeem ourselves from our sin but God intervened on our behalf. He again worked for His creation and made a way for us to be redeemed and to be reconciled to Him. He has not just paid the price for our sins but He has actually released us from our slavery to sin. If all He had done was to pay for our sins that would be enough to be excited about but He did so much more than just provide forgiveness. He made it possible for us, through the Holy Spirit, to live a life saying no to sin. He made it possible, to live a life for Him, by living by His principle and laws. He actually made it possible to be a true disciple.

You may have thought when reading the previous chapter of this book that you could not live a life completely devoted to Him but that is exactly what He made possible. In our own strength we could not do that but with the Holy Spirit, we can do everything God requires of us.

So do you still want to refer to yourselves as just sinners saved by grace? Let us look at whom the Bible says we are when we are in Jesus. ***"To all in Rome who are loved by God and called to be his holy people: Grace and peace to you from God our Father and from the Lord Jesus Christ" (Romans 1:7)***. This is a common greeting Paul gives at the beginning of his letters to various churches. Imagine how you would change your daily interactions with others if you were to remember you are loved by God and called to be saints. We are not called to live a pathetic existence, we are called to be saints, and whether we realize it or not, that is what we are when we are in Christ. Paul wrote two letters to the church at Corinth. This was a church that had problems. Does that sound familiar? Yet he still refers to them as saints. We tend to think of someone as a saint because of something they have done but the fact is that we are saints not because of what we have done but because of what God has done on our behalf. In Ephesians, Philippians, and Colossians he starts off the letters by referring to the people of God as saints.

When you take a look at the first chapter of Ephesians it is amazing the picture that is given of the believer. In verse 3, we are told we are blessed by God with every spiritual blessing. In verse 4, we are told that we have been chosen before the foundation of the world. It goes on to tell us that we are to be holy and without blame before Him. The next verse tells us, we were predestined for adoption as sons. Verse 7, tells us of the redemption we have through His blood and the forgiveness of sin. Verse 9, reminds us, He has made known the mystery of His will. According to verse 11, we have been given an inheritance. I would say that we are much more than just a simple sinner saved by grace. In Christ we are truly children of the King. We have been adopted into the family of the creator of the universe. Not only are we part of His family but He has chosen to use us to complete His mission. All this was done because He loves me not because I deserve it, in fact I do not really deserve it but He has chosen to redeem me.

If we took the time to examine everything in scripture that God thinks about us we would have to write a separate book from this one. The word of God tells us much about who we are in Jesus, and remember we are talking those that are His disciples. All who we are is because of the work of Jesus so when we realize it is all a result of His work there will be no fear of us becoming prideful.

We hear so much talk today about self-esteem and how important it is for us to live a healthy life. It is of great value for a person to have a good self-esteem but the problem becomes where we get it from. When it becomes about us, and what we have accomplished, it becomes something that will have highs and lows, as we go through the seasons of our lives. When we base our self-esteem on what Jesus has done for us, what He thinks about us, what He has made us into it will be something that never changes because God's opinion of us does not change. How much more self-esteem can you have when you are a child of the King? How much more value can you place on your life than to have the creator of the universe love you, care for you , have his son die for you and to have Him actually use you to complete His work on this earth? If our teens could get a hold of this truth they would find it easier to stand up to the enemy of their souls.

As you turn the page and go to the next chapter I want you to do so while keeping this in your mind and in your heart. We were at one time sinners and we were at enmity with God. But if you are a Christian you now have been forgiven by God, and He no longer views you as His enemy. You have now, become a child of the king, you are a friend of God, you are a member of a chosen race, a royal priesthood, you are God's own possession, and you have been made complete in Christ. The creator of the universe is taking care of you.

Questions for Reflection

1. How did you see yourself when you were younger and what role did others views play in your view of yourself?

2. How did that change when you came to Christ?

3. How has that change affected your day to day actions?

Mark Tollefson

4

Don't Worry...Trust God

"Therefore I tell you, do not worry about your life, what you will eat or drink; or about your body, what you will wear. Is not life more than food and the body more than clothes?"

Matthew 6:25

This (Matthew 6:25) seems like a straight forward statement. It seems like it would be simple to understand. I would imagine there would be no room for argument with this statement; after all it came straight from Jesus. In fact if you look at this statement in its proper context it becomes even clearer that there is no reason to worry when we follow the one true God. If only life were that simple—life should be when we follow God.

This is one of those areas that I hear people use the 'but statement', it goes something like this: I know I should not worry but I am only human. I know I should not worry but I just cannot stop worrying. I know I should not worry but it helps me be motivated to do something. I know we are not supposed to worry but it shows that I care. Do any of these sound familiar? They are, of course, all just hollow excuses that do not hold water. They are just ways we think will justify our sinful behaviour.

This may be the biggest area which Christians struggle with and usually fail miserably when it comes to putting it into practice. The world will look at us, and will see that when we are going through the same struggles that we worry all the same, why would they ask us about our hope? When they do not see any hope in us? All they see is a person that says they trust God but is doing everything the same way as they would approach the struggle. The question that we face here and we need to analyze is why is this so? It is one thing to realize we have an issue but if we do not look at the root and discover why we are in the state we are then how can we get to the point where we correct wrong behaviour? It seems to me that many people seem to be happy to admit their shortcomings but that is where they stop. They refuse, once they realize they have a problem to look for a cause and a solution.

As I reflect on the current malaise in this area and what has caused it, I realize one issue is exactly what happened to the Corinthian church. We have let the world's thinking enter the Church. Instead of us influencing the world the world has changed the way we see things, even the way we see the Bible, and the principles God has given us to live by. It is like looking at everything through shaded glasses. Depending on the colour of glass the world looks differently and when it looks differently we react in a way that we would not if we were looking through the proper lenses. The proper lens would be the Bible and when we look at the world with what is called a Biblical worldview everything changes. We all of a sudden can keep things in perspective and we will know exactly how to handle any situation.

When reflecting on this, what comes to mind is the verse, **"For you have been my refuge, a strong tower against the foe" (Psalms 61:3).** If you look at this verse in its historic context you will realize a tower performed at least two functions for the one that ran into it and used it for safety. First, it provided a literal wall that your enemy would have to breach to be able to do you harm, no matter what weapon they had it would somehow have to get through that wall.

Secondly, the other protection it afforded was what directly applies to this area. When one climbed to the top of the tower it provided the one under its protection with a different view of the battle. The person could then see what was happening all around them and would then be better able to determine a plan of action. This is precisely what God and His Word provides for us. When we look at the world the way he sees it and with a perspective of eternity, we tend to act completely different than the way those that are non-Christians would respond to any given situation. When we let the world's thinking slip into the church we can start to even tell the Gospel a different way. When we keep our eyes on God's way, we will be able to present a living example of God's word to the world around us that is desperate for good news.

I want to look at a few worldly attitudes that have crept into the church and which have affected our ability to really have the victory over the problem of worry. After, I will share the seven practical steps to eradicating worry in your life. We need to be constantly examining our lives to see if the world's way of thinking is affecting the Biblical worldview we need to have to show the love of Christ to others so they will see that we have a hope in us and will actually ask what it is all about.

The first attitude is control. The thing people who are not following God seem really to covet is to have complete control over their lives. People really hate it when they lose that control and they see that someone else is actually in control of their destiny. We can clearly see this when it comes to the crime that is active in our country. One big issue when it comes to this, whether it is local crime, like getting your car stolen or your house broke into or it involves terrorism, the big thing which people lose is the control over their belongings and themselves. That is why with a house break-in, you hear the victims talking about the feelings of violation and helplessness. What they are saying is that they had no control over who entered their property. It is the fear of the unknown, we never know when we walk down the street what to expect. Look at the great lengths we go to in order to get back that control. We can spend large amounts of money to install alarms or high tech locks in our homes and businesses all in an effort to gain back some control. We are even glad to give up some of our own rights to give the illusion we have some control over what is happening to us.

When we look at lotteries or any get rich quick scheme we can see the issue of control. In reality, that is what the American dream is all about. If you work hard and pull up your bootstraps you can make something of yourselves. What they are really saying is if you work hard, you can call the shots, and be the one in control. Just look at what people say would happen to them if they won the big lottery. If I win this much money I would be able to buy this, do that, go here, and then I would really be happy. They really believe that the key to being happy is to have complete control over their life. They do not want to have to answer to anyone; they do not want the "man" to control them. Really that is what anarchy is all about. In actuality the opposite is true and the way to really have an abundant life is to give up that control to God. We will talk about that in more detail later.

One other area that the world's way of doing and thinking has crept into the church is our picture of God. We will talk about this at length in another chapter in the book. For now though we need to realize that the non-Christian has a view of God that is very un-biblical and it is almost becoming the norm for the people who call themselves Christians to have the same thoughts about God. Many people think that God is some force out there but He is not a personal God that is interested in every aspect of their lives. They have a very small view of God. This kind of thinking has come into the church so much that when God does something even small we seem to be amazed that he can and would do that.

When was the last time that God did something really big? Whether it was a healing, maybe meeting a huge financial need, or maybe saving a loved one that had been wandering for years? When that happened, did you marvel at the greatness of God? He is great and we should marvel at Him. At the same time did you feel like the following statement: Of course, He did that, do you realize who God is?

When my wife returned to school for nursing a few years back she was not sure that she could accomplish her goal but she stepped out in faith trusting God. When she received the mark for her first exam I had gotten into a bit of trouble because when she told me how well she had done, I really did not have much of a reaction. When she asked me why, I explained to her that I knew she was capable of doing well so it was no surprise to me to see her achieve an excellent mark. This is the way we need to think of God, of course He can do that. I am not saying we should not marvel at his mercy and certainly be in awe of Him but we need to start expecting Him to do great things, just like I expected my wife to do great things in school.

Our view of God and Satan has been skewed by popular culture, TV, and media. Even those that go to church see God as an old man sitting on some throne in heaven and they see the devil as some little guy in a red suit with a pitchfork. If you think I am stretching things here just ask people in the church who is in charge of hell, and you may get a surprising answer. It is amazing how little knowledge we have of the God that is revealed to us through the pages of scripture. We seem to have a real lack of knowledge of the word of God and therefore we are easily influenced by what the world tells us about whom God is; therefore, we sometimes do not believe that He is able to see us through and we really have no need of worry.

When we really look at it we know that worry serves absolutely no positive purpose. In fact it will actually do us a lot of harm. If you read any study on the subject you will see it can cause us both physical and psychological harm. Just think, for a minute about this one example. You have a teenage child and they are out with their friends. You have set the curfew and you really have no concern about them making home by curfew because they always have respected that and have always been home on time. So why is it that many parents will worry about the child being out and they will stay up until they arrive safely home? What good has it done to stay up? Will the act of worrying actually keep them from any harm? Is the act of staying up to worry what brought them home safe? The reality is that when that child is out of the house with their friends they are out of the parent's control. There is that word again. Plenty of parents do not seem comfortable with leaving their children in God's hands; they somehow think that they can do a better job if they "help" God out.

I am sure you have heard sermons on the subject of worry and you have had the pastor stand in front of you and tell you how you should not worry. He will have quoted scripture on the subject of worry. He may even tell you that it is exhibiting a lack of faith when we worry. Then he may give you stories of how someone had worried about something and then everything had turned out all right, at least it turned out how they wanted and he will use that for example of why not to worry. He may even use some statistics about what we worry about and how useless it is to drive his point home. They may tell you that a certain percentage of things we worry about never happen and that is supposed to mean we are wasting our time worrying. What about the times what we were worrying about actually happened, does that mean it was okay to worry about that? I would say definitely not. All these approaches are well meaning and meant to motivate you and direct you into a positive pattern. But the fact is whether we worry or not, everything does not work out how we would like it to, sometimes we will go through hardships. After a sermon with a focus on worry, we fully intend on putting it into practice but the reality is that we have just scratched the surface, and when we get to Monday, all we have learned, and intended to do has worn off.

So how do we effectively defeat worry? I have in the next chapter, seven practical steps to eradicating worry. I fully believe that if you follow all these steps you can conquer worry in your life and live victoriously. Then when troubles come and your friend and family see the way you react to them they will truly see the hope that is in you. Then, they will be motivated to ask you about that hope. I know that it is a bold statement to make that these steps will work in your life but I can make that statement because the following steps are simply based on Godly principles laid out in Scripture.

Questions for Reflection

1. How has worry improved your life? Yes that is a trick question.

2. Why do you believe you must worry?

3. Why is it wrong to worry?

4. What does Jesus tell us about worry?

There Are No Buts Except The One You Are Sitting On

5

Defeating Worry

Step One

Knowing Who God Is

The first step is something we have already talked about and that is for you to really know who God is and what He is like. This cannot be some kind of abstract view of God; it cannot be just something you have heard as you grew up or something that you hear from popular culture. If you just know God as the guy upstairs or some old man with a beard sitting on a throne, or maybe as some kind of God sitting somewhere waiting for you to mess up so he can punish you, then you will never be able completely to trust Him. Would you trust someone you hardly know to watch your children for a week, while you went out of town? No, you would not.

Before we go any farther I want you to take a minute and think about whom God is and what you think you know about Him. Take some time before you go any farther and even write on a piece of paper what you really know, about God, and how you found out about Him. Now I want you to take some more time to think of someone in your life that is important to you and someone who you know well. Do the same thing you did for God, write down somewhere, what you know about them, and how you found this information out about them.

I would guess that you know a lot more about that special person in your life than you do God. There are various ways that you have gotten to know that person; it will have mostly come from interacting with them. Some of the information you will have learned from other people, but most of what you know, about that person, you found out through your own observations.

Why do you know more about that person? Well, it is because that person is so important to you. You have taken the time to study them, you have watched them, you have talked to them, and you probably have asked them questions about themselves to learn what they like and what they do not like. You have spent time with them.

If the person you thought of was someone who you do not personally know but someone who you looked up to and someone who has affected your life you have probably taken time to study about them. You may have read a book about them, you may have watched a show on TV about them or maybe you typed their name into Google to find out more information about them. The more you know someone the more you will trust them, the more you will depend on them. The better you know them the more likely you are to take what they say at face value and just accept what they are saying as reliable. Are you getting the picture yet?

We need to study God in that way and even more than that, after all He should be the most important person in our lives bar none. We need to take time to learn everything we possibly can about the attributes of God. At one point in the adult Sunday school class at my church we went through a series on the attributes of God. It was a lengthy series because there was so much to learn about Him. I had told the class that when you learn about whom God is that should excite us and it has to change you and the way you behave. If it does not affect your everyday walk with God then, there is something wrong.

Here are some of the attributes of God; independent, unchangeable, eternal, omnipresent, spiritual, omniscient, invisible, wise, faithful, good, love, mercy, grace, patience, peace, holy, jealous, righteous, wrath, has a will, powerful, omnipotent. Let us look at just a few of these, and see how, when we understand them, how they could be applied to us conquering worry.

God is unchangeable, he is always the same, we do not have to worry that one day He will require something of us and then the next day He will change His mind. Hebrew 13:8 tells us, **"Jesus Christ is the same yesterday and today and forever."** This is just one verse that tells us God does not change. Just think about that for a moment God has never changed, he remains a constant. How many things in your life can you say that about? We as people change, we change as we get older, we change as we grow in the Lord, we change in what we like and we do not like but God stays the same forever. There has never been a time that He has not been exactly what He is now. He, unlike us, did not have to mature into who He is now He just always was. Remember when Moses asked Him, who that he should say that He is, and God just replied tell them "I am".

When it comes to defeating worry can you imagine a better person to put your complete and absolute trust in then a God that never changes? Just think about someone who you know that you have put some trust in. Maybe, you have left them with a task and you were confident that they would complete the task. From their side they had every intention of doing it for you but in the busyness of life they changed their mind and did something else. Would you trust them again? Well you might but the next time you would be wondering if they were going to do what they said they would do. You may even keep an eye on them to make sure they did what they said. Well that is not what our God is about, when He promises something in the Bible you can rest assured it will be done. When he says you can cast all your cares on Him that is what he means, He will not change His mind and leave you because something else came up. We may change, our lives may change, but God never changes. Do you really think you have to worry about anything when that is the God we serve?

God is wise. ***Isaiah 55:8-9, "For my thoughts are not your thoughts, neither are your ways my ways, saith the Lord. For as the heavens are higher than the earth, so are my ways higher than your ways, and my thoughts than your thoughts"***. We could stop right there with that verse but let me share another with you from Romans. **Romans 11:33-34, "O the depth of the riches both of the wisdom and knowledge of God! How unsearchable are his judgments, and his ways past finding out! For who hath known the mind of the Lord?**

Or who hath been his counselor?" These again are just two verses. There are other verses that talk about God's great wisdom as well. I just want you to meditate on these two scriptures for a moment and get the full impact of what God is telling us about Himself. It is not just that He is a smart God, but rather, His wisdom far surpasses ours. We cannot even compare our minds with His. We do not even come close to His wisdom and knowledge.

We cannot even imagine His thoughts. Remember He knows the beginning from the end; He does not have to look back at what happened to figure out what to do next, He already knows what is coming. Remember we talked about having the view from the tower where we can see the overall picture, well that is the closest we can come to understanding how God sees the world. This is how He sees us. He can look down through time and act based on what he knows is going to happen. It is not like we do when we look ahead and plan the best we can for what we think is going to happen, He acts based on what He knows will happen, after all He is in control of the future, the present, and the past. Nothing happens that surprises Him.

Have you ever had the experience where something happened and you thought, wow I did not see that coming? He never has that feeling, nothing is beyond

His control. In fact Psalms says, **"Our God is in heaven; he does whatever pleases him" (Psalms 115:3).**

It is amazing to me how much we look up to people in society that we consider to be smart. They may be in the world or they may be in the church. If they sound intelligent we will listen even more. Just think about your favourite news anchor on TV or you favourite talk radio host. Now think about how much you trust them, think about the fact that if you hear them tell you something you will generally trust them and not question the facts. Now compare their wisdom to the wisdom of God. Remember the two verses we just used. Who do you think is more trustworthy?

I believe we can see from this that because God is wise we can confidently leave our future, our children's future, and anyone we care about in the Lord's hands, and not be concerned whatsoever. His will is going to be done no matter what.

These are just two of God's attributes. We just quickly went through them but you could spend a much longer time looking at just these two. In the interest of time I have just examined it quickly to give you an idea of what to do. I suggest you take time and carefully go through your Bible and learn all you can about God, and you will quickly see it has to change the way you look at the things you are worrying about.

I would caution you about going too fast in studies like this so that you do not just do it to confirm what you think you already know about God. Do it in a way that you can be learning new things about the God of Creation, the God that provided for your salvation. This is not intended as a ten minute Bible devotion before you start your day it needs to be a study that is intended to change your life and your faith walk. If you stopped at step one you would be long on your way to conquering worry. But do not stop here we are just getting started.

Step Two

Memorize Appropriate Bible Verses

I will probably state this in more than one step but this is an important step. Do not under estimate its importance. This does seem to be one area of Bible study we have lost somewhat. There was a time when Bible memorization was done routinely but that seems to be something we have lost along the way. I do not want to go into why we have lost this skill but we do need to start realizing the role it can play in our faith walk.

When times of struggle come whether it be about worrying or any other struggle we have in our life we will not always have a Bible handy to look though to find a verse that would go with the particular situation. Imagine you are driving the highway and you are worrying about something that you should be leaving to God you cannot exactly pull out a Bible and start reading. But when you have key verses memorize the Holy Spirit will bring them to you mind at that time and you will be reminded of God's promises to you, or you may be reminded of one of His attributes that enables you fully to trust Him with your situation.

I will give you one cautionary note here before I continue and that is about taking verses out of their original context. It is said that in real estate the location is everything, well when it comes to understanding the Bible, context is extremely important to proper understanding. Too many times I hear a verse being quoted and used to explain something or apply to a particular situation, on analysis you can look at the context and see that it was never intended to be used that way. My advice would be that when you go to memorize a particular scripture, study it and find out what it really means and how it applies to your life. When doing this remember to look at three types of context. The first is the biblical context, second is the historic context, and thirdly the cultural context. When you take a little time to do this you will find that scripture really comes alive for you.

I would like to now relate a personal story to you of how this principle has been lived out in my life. There was a time when I was consumed by worry, if there was nothing to be worried about I could think of something to be upset about. We live in an older house with a steep gable roof and our bedroom at the time was upstairs. The bedroom upstairs is simply a converted attic, so when the bed was against the wall, the roof started just a bit above the bed. One day my wife being concerned about the fact that I was worrying and not following the principles laid out in the Bible decided to do something about it. She got some paper and hand wrote several verses on the paper and taped them to the roof directly over my side of the bed. Every night as I was getting ready to get into bed and as I was lying there I came face to face with the word of God. All the verses that she had taken the time to copy down and tape up there were about how I did not need to worry and about completely trusting God for all my needs.

To be honest the results were not immediate but after time it sank in to my mind and my heart. I could no longer come up with excuses of why those verses were for a different situation. After time, it got to the point that when I would want to worry, those verses were so ingrained in me they would come to my mind first and to ignore them would have been disobedience to God. Who was I to argue with the creator of the universe? What comes to mind when I reflect on this is from the Psalms. **"I have hidden your word in my heart that I might not sin against you" (Psalm 119:11)**. The best way to follow God is to first know what He has said, and then have His word in your heart, so that when the struggles come the default position will be to rely on His word and obey that word.

There are many verses in the Bible that deal with this issue and I would like to share a few of them with you, as my wife did with me those years ago. This is certainly not an exhaustive list but is a sampling. As I suggested in Step One take these verses and conduct a deeper study to gather more.

- Matthew 6:25-34
- Colossians 3:15
- 1 Peter 5:7
- Hebrews 13:6
- Romans 8:31

"Do not be anxious about anything, but in every situation, by prayer and petition, with thanksgiving,

present your requests to God. And the peace of God, which transcends all understanding, will guard your hearts and your minds in Christ Jesus" (Philippians 4:6-7).** This is a special verse for me because of what Paul went through in his life. If anyone had a reason to worry it would be Paul. As it says in 2 Corinthians 11:25-29, he went through beatings, imprisonment, he had been stoned, he was shipwrecked and in danger from his own people. Do you think he had anything to worry about? Through all this, Paul knew his strength came from the Lord and he did not have to worry because God was in charge of his life.

Step Three

Know your History

It has been said that those that do not know history are doomed to repeat it. This has been shown time and time again with the human race. We all have a history and we can all look back and see the things that God has brought us through. If you are reading this book it is a testament to God's grace that you are still here no matter how much you have gone through. You may think that because you have had a tough life that God has somehow let you down. Really the opposite is true, if you have been through horrendous events in your life, and God has brought you this far it means you can trust Him to take you to the end.

There are different ways to do this but the first one is to keep a prayer journal. This does take a little discipline but it is worth the effort. It gives you a chance to look back over the years and see how God has answered prayer. It may surprise you the way God has worked in your life, He does things His way, and that can be an amazing thing to look back on. I believe we can admit this but there are very few of us that actually keep prayer journals, I know some do and that is great but here is another idea of how to remember your history.

Take some time and sit down and just start off by thinking about your life. Think about where you have been the places you have gone, the people who God has brought into your life, and the good and bad times. After you have spent some time doing this take out your computer or some paper and write down your history. It can be in point form, or you can do it like you are writing a book, or even a short story. Once you have done this keep it in a place where it will be safe but at the same time you can easily find it and read it often. This will be a reference point for you when you think that it is time to worry about something, take it out and read it and remember the faithfulness of God.

Next we can also look to the Bible to help us in this step. The Bible is full of stories of God's faithfulness to His people. It is extremely important for you to make time to study the Bible. You can read stories of God's interaction with His creation, after all that is what the whole book is about. God has written the history of His faithfulness throughout the generations. It is an amazing thing to look at the way God has brought us through but it is amazing to realize he has done this since the beginning of time. Read the stories of Abraham, Moses, King David, Paul and all the apostles just to mention a few. Look at Hebrews 11, and read the great people of faith, and see what God has done for them. Remember to read the whole chapter, the great victories, and the times events did not work out as we would think they should. But God was with everyone and every story ends in Victory with Jesus.

God reminds us of this step in Deuteronomy. **"Teach them to your children, talking about them when you sit at home and when you walk along the road, when you lie down and when you get up. Write them on the door frames of your houses and on your gates, so that your days and the days of your children may be many in the land the Lord swore to give your ancestors, as**

many as the days that the heavens are above the Earth" (Deuteronomy 11:18-21). In this section, He is talking about the words of God and yet the same concept would follow with what God has done for us. At various times, the people of Israel were instructed after a great victory to construct a monument, so that when people asked them why it was there they could remind them of the great victory God had won. In fact that is when the people of Israel would go astray, when they forgot that all they had come from was because of God and the fact they followed His ways. So when we are tempted to worry about something we need to remember our History. When we realize what God has done for us how can we not simply put our trust in Him?

Step Four

Practice

In North America we have become spoiled. We have so much and we have access to so much at times we feel we can do everything ourselves. We at times have a Christianity that is really more about us than it is about Christ. We feel we can do anything, solve any problem with our own methods, instead of trusting is God to take us through it. We make it so we are just taking God along for the journey but it is up to us to make all the decisions. When that becomes our focus it is inevitable that we will mess it up at some point. It is only because of the grace of God that we do not crash and burn sooner than it usually happens.

We have been actually taught by our parents and by society that it is up to us to make our own way and fulfill our own destiny. Even in Christian homes a lot of the times the focus is on us and how we can make our way. There is a belief that if we just pull up our bootstraps and work hard everything will be okay. We seem to have adopted this approach in our walk with God as well. Then when it does not work out as we assume it should we blame God. Now do not get me wrong here, I am certainly not against having a work ethic, and God does expect us to work hard. He expects us to give our all, but we need to give our all to Him first, not to ourselves. When we became Christians, we gave up the kingship of our lives, and turned it over to Christ.

This whole attitude transfers over to the problem of worry. Whenever something comes up that we cannot immediately understand or we do not know how it will turn out the first response we have is, what can I do to make it work? Or we ask what did we do wrong or if I do not do the right thing it will all fail as it all relies on me. Where is God in that frame of mind? This even happens in church ministries, when we feel the success of a particular program, it is about how we did it instead of what does God want us to do with the effort.

We need to have the mindset that God is not a last resort; instead He needs to be the first responder. If you have a heart attack the first phone call you make will be to 911, it will not be to check your bank balance. The only way this will happen is if we make it a habit to put God at the top of the list not at the bottom. We need to remember that good habits are still habits. I do not mean we put Him at the top of the list we turn to when we have a problem, He needs to be number one when everything seems to be going great, and number one when things seem to be falling apart.

We have a tendency in today's culture to compartmentalize our lives. We feel this part of our life is for our wife, this is for my children, and this is the part I give to my job and so on. We seem to think if we can just give the right size of the pie to each activity everything will be fine. The problem is that this worldly attitude has come into our walk with God and that He is just another piece of the overall pie. This is not what God intended at all. He needs to be the whole pie as it were. He cannot just be a part of our lives He must be our whole lives. He cannot be our number one priority He must be everything and then we can rank the rest of our lives. So when it comes to something we feel we need to be worrying about God is not just the first thing we try. He is the only answer and we need to let Him direct our ways and do what we must but always with the mindset that it is the Lord that gives and takes away. It is the Lord that is in complete control of our lives and the outcomes of our plans.

The next time you are faced with a situation that you are worried about stop and take a moment to take stock of what you are doing. When you realize how the worry is affecting you pray and tell God you are going to trust Him for the results, you do not trust Him for the results you want. Instead you are going to trust that He does know what He is doing and allow Him to work in the situation. After time, of seeing, and allowing God to work on your behalf, and have His way in your life, it will be easier leave the results up to Him. Soon it will become a habit and it will be your first response, not your last one when you have run out of options.

Step Five

Pray Expectantly

If you want to buy a car you may first do some research on different models and then decide which one would best suit your needs. Or maybe you have come to a point in your life where you can buy your dream car. So you go down to your local car dealer and you make the best deal you can to obtain the car in the colour you want with the options you desire. Then you tell the sales rep that you want it in blue. Well apparently that is a problem because there are no blue ones on the lot. The sales rep tells you that it is no problem because he can order you one. So you pay your deposit and sign all the papers and go home.

Once you go home do you then start to worry that they will not order your car or maybe they just will not get it for you because they do not feel like doing it for you. Of course not, you fully expect that the sales rep will fulfill his end of the contract, and at some point you will be driving in your new car. All you have to do is to wait and have a little faith in the sales rep.

Generally speaking, we do not have much of a struggle to have the faith in another person doing what they said they would do, especially if we know them. So why is it that we do not seem to have the same faith in God? That sales rep is only doing something for you because there is a paycheck in it for him; it is not because he actually cares about your wellbeing. How much more should we expect God to act on our behalf when He actually cares about us, and humanity itself? He does it because of His great love for us. God, unlike that sales rep actually wants the best for us. The sales rep will give us what we want because we are paying him to act on our behalf. God is doing it out of concern for us; Jesus told us He came to give us life abundantly. When we know that He cares that much about us and those around us it should be natural for us to expect Him to act On our behalf.

Let us look at what James has to say, about us praying this way, **"If any of you lacks wisdom, you should ask**

God, who gives generously to all without finding fault, and it will be given to you. But when you ask, you must believe and not doubt, because the one who doubts is like a wave of the sea, blown and tossed by the wind. That person should not expect to receive anything from the Lord. Such a person is double-minded and unstable in all they do" (James 1:5-8). And a little later he tells us, **"when you ask, you do not receive; because you ask with wrong motives, that you may spend what you get on your pleasures" (James 4:3).**

So what is James telling us in these scriptures? He is saying in the first case that if we need wisdom all we have to do is to ask God. But then he adds that when you ask expect that He will answer that prayer and if you do not expect then you are double minded you should expect to receive nothing. Remember he says we should not expect to receive anything it does not mean we definitely will not just that why should we expect to get something when we really do not have the faith that God will actually do it. I believe that problem is that when we really do not expect to receive it from God then we generally go about our own way trying other methods to get something that we should be getting from God. We somehow think we have to help God along as if He was not capable of doing it without our help. In the second verse He tells us that when we ask we sometimes do not receive because we ask with wrong motives. Our motives are about ourselves instead of the about the kingdom of God. When you put the two verses together, remember we need to look at context, we see that if we ask with the right motives then we should expect to receive from God.

When we pray for someone do we really expect God to act or do we just pray because we think that is what we should do and we think that is all we can do? When we pray for a friend, or loved one, that is sick, or struggling, do we follow up on it? What we should be doing is to pray and then wait to hear how God has acted on the person's behalf. We do not need to ask timidly how they are, hoping that maybe there is some good news but instead we need to ask expecting to hear something great that God has done. It may not be what we expected but it will be what God wanted to do and that is always the best thing. When we ask God let us move away from the attitude of I hope God has heard my prayer and I hope He answers. Let us move to the attitude, I know God has heard my cry and I cannot wait to see how he will act in this situation.

Step Six

Leave Your Burdens with God

When you take your car into to be repaired what do you do? The first thing you will most likely do is go into the service department and tell the service attendant there, exactly what is going on with your car. You probably will not know exactly what is going wrong but you will know the symptoms, you will know what you feel it should be driving like. The service attendant may ask you several questions to get a better idea of the problem and the mechanic may even come out and talk to you so he has an idea of what is going wrong. It will also allow him to know where to start looking for the problem. Once this is done they will write up some kind of service order outlining the problem and get you to sign it giving them permission to work on your car. Sometimes they may know what is wrong with the car just from your description and be able to tell you what they need to do and give you a price. At this point you will give them the keys and walk out of the place and leave the car with them.

It would be pretty silly of you to go through the process and then take the car keys with you and expect them to fix it without the keys. They would have to call you back and get the keys so they could repair the vehicle. It would make even less sense if you took the whole car home with you and still thought that they could fix it without actually having the car there. No, you have to leave the car and the keys behind with them, you have to leave the problem behind and allow them to come up with a solution to fix it.

So why is it that when we pray about a situation that we seem to get up from that prayer and pick our burden back up and carry it with us? How do you expect God to work when you will not give Him the keys to your life? This goes hand in hand with the previous step. When you pray expectantly you need to get up off your knees and let Him have it all. In the words of Jesus **"Come to me, all you who are weary and burdened, and I will give you rest" (Matthew 11:28).**

This does not mean that you play no role in it what so ever. It is not that you pray and then throw your hands up in the air and do absolutely nothing. You have to do what is necessary and then let God bring the results. When my daughter was 16, she went on a mission's trip to Nigeria. There was a lot of preparation to do before she actually boarded the plane. We had to make sure she had the money to go; she had to get immunizations to combat infections of different types. We bought her travel insurance and she packed various things that would be useful on a trip of this type. She also had to purchase an air plane ticket to get there. For the people in Nigeria, there was preparation on their part to get ready for the arrival of the team she was going with. We did what we could do for her to have a successful trip.

But when all was said and done the results of that trip was not up to us. We had to leave our daughter in the hands of God. For us to do all those preparations and then sit back and worry about her everyday would have done absolutely no good. We did our part but the reality is that God was in complete control all the time. The question of whether or not she would make it back safely or not was up to the creator of the universe. I know there is no better place for our daughter to be than in the hands of the one that loved us all enough to send His son to die so that we could be reconciled to Him. We had to leave everything to God. Like the car example at the beginning of this section we did not know exactly what was going to happen in Nigeria, however, we knew God was in control.

I was told by a friend of a meeting they went to where the speaker had told them to write their need down on a piece of paper. They were told to pray about the need and when they left the altar to leave that piece of paper behind. This was a symbolic gesture but the message was powerful. When they left that building they were to leave those needs in the hands of God. This is what we need to do every time we pray.

We need to practice doing this so this too becomes a habit. Maybe you can, like the example I gave, try writing, that need on a piece of paper and when you are finished praying leave it somewhere, maybe crumble it up and throw it away symbolizing you are leaving it with God. The first time you do this a while later it may come to your mind that you must worry about that again. That is exactly what Satan wants you to do. At that point you need to rebuke him and make a conscious decision not to own that again. You need to make a choice not to dwell on the need; you need to again immediately turn to God in prayer. Ask Him to forgive you for wanting to pick that burden up and then leave it with Him again. You may need to at this point, remind yourself of the character of God, or maybe think about your history, or maybe even go through all seven steps right at that time. Do not just go on and try to blow it off, take time to leave it with God no matter how long it takes. It may take a bit, before you are actually able to leave it with God, but do not get discouraged, as it is all part of spiritual discipline.

Just like when you start exercising it takes a while to work up to a heavy workout it may take a bit to get to the point where you can actually leave everything with

God. But as Paul talked about keeping your eyes on the prize when running race, keep your eyes and heart on what you are doing. The victory you will enjoy when you practice spiritual discipline will be worth any amount of time and effort you put into the process.

Step Seven

Give Up Control

This is similar to the last step and goes hand in hand with it. The reason it is so hard to leave our burdens with God is because doing that means we have to give up control of the outcome and are forced to accept what God wants to do in any situation. Of course the reality is that the way God wants to do it is always the best way. At times we may not see how it is the best way but remember I did not say the best way for you. God knows the end from the beginning and He is working His plan out so therefore He knows what is best in any situation. It is amazing how much better we feel when we actually give up control. If we could just realize that in reality God is always in control anyway. When you really think about it, when we give up the control in our lives it really does take the pressure off of us because then, although we must do our part, the results are up to God.

I believe it is especially hard for men to give up the control to anyone. We are raised to be the problem solvers. Society tells us it is a sign of weakness to let someone else control your life, whether it is another person or God. Men are taught to challenge anyone that tries to take that control away from them. By the worlds standards if a man seems like he is not in complete control of his destiny he is considered to be weak. How many times have you heard Christianity called a crutch? It is because of this, that it is hard to admit that something is beyond your control. The world has turned us into a bunch of control freaks. There are many passages in the Bible that reminds us of the fact that God is in complete control and I would like to share a few with you now. The first one is **from Psalm 139,**

you perceive my thoughts from afar. You discern my going out and my lying down; you are familiar with all

my ways. Before a word is on my tongue you, Lord, know it completely. You hem me in behind and before, and you lay your hand upon me. Such knowledge is too wonderful for me, too lofty for me to attain. Where can I go from your Spirit? Where can I flee from your presence? If I go up to the heavens, you are there; if I make my bed in the depths, you are there. If I rise on the wings of the dawn, if I settle on the far side of the sea, even there your hand will guide me; your right hand will hold me fast. If I say, 'Surely the darkness will hide me and the light become night around me,' even the darkness will not be dark to you; the night will shine like the day, for darkness is as light to you."

This is the God we are trying to wrestle control from and some people actually demand the control from Him. Why we want to take control from someone who knows us like this? Is it not fair to say that a God that knows these things would certainly be able to take care of us and know what is best for us?

I have always enjoyed the story of Joseph and the lessons we can learn from it. As you may know, Joseph was the favourite child of Jacob, because this, and his dreams his brothers did not like him. To make a long story short, his brothers devised a plan to get rid of him, eventually selling him into slavery, where Joseph ended in Egypt. He served time at Potiphar's house and then because of the Potiphar's wife ended in jail. After years in jail, he then became second in command in Egypt, specifically, in charge of storing food for the coming famine. When the famine came his family was forced to come to him to buy food. In this way God kept His people alive through the famine.

When Joseph revealed himself to his brothers they were very afraid. Joseph said to them, **"Don't be afraid. Am I in the place of God? You intended to harm me, but God intended it for good to accomplish what is now being done, the saving of many lives" (Genesis 50:19-20)**. It is an incredible thing to think that his brothers thought they were in control when they committed this act but all the time God was going to use it to save the people of Israel. We need to realize that the longer we want to control the situation the harder it will be to give up worry. You may not realize that control is a problem for you but that really is why we worry because we face a situation with unknown results, therefore, we get concerned how it will play out. We always need to remember that, although, we may not know how we are going to pay our bills, or if our loved one will recover, or even where our next meal will come from, God has it all figured out already so there is not point to worry about what tomorrow will bring because God holds tomorrow in His hand.

Questions for Reflection

1.   Which if of seven steps do you find the most difficult to implement and why?

2.   Do you really believe that living a life without worry is possible?

3.   Do you really believe you can do a better job at controlling situations than God, if not why do we want to wrestle control from Him?

There Are No Buts Except The One You Are Sitting On

6

Forgiveness

"For if you forgive men when they sin against you, your heavenly Father will also forgive you. But if you do not forgive men their sins, your Father will not forgive your sins."

Matthew 6:14-15

This is a harsh way to start a chapter but I want you to take a minute and really let these words of Jesus sink in to your heart and your mind. Can you imagine a harsher reality then this that God will not forgive us if we do not forgive others? Is there anyone in your life that you have not forgiven? Is there someone in your life that because of your attitude toward them God will not forgive you?

This is an area of life that many Christians seem to struggle with in their daily walk with God. It seems we are very good at living our daily lives while blocking out the areas of our lives that are not pleasing to God. We can just simply write someone off and harbour un-forgiveness and live our lives as if we are model Christians. We make it into an area of our lives that seems unimportant, after all we feel that person was in the wrong and he or she does not really matter in my life anyway. How many Christians are sitting in the churches while on the other side of the church is a person they have not forgiven. We are there worshiping God yet we are harbouring a grudge against our brother or sister. God takes it a lot more seriously than we seem to take this issue of forgiveness.

In Matthew chapter five Jesus is talking about murder and equates being angry with your brother in the same thought. Next time they pass the offering plate around in your churches think about the words of Christ here in Matthew 5. *"Therefore, if you are offering your gift at the altar and there remember that your brother has something against you, leave your gift there in front of the altar. First go and be reconciled to your brother; then come and offer your gift." (Matthew 5:23-24)*

This is another area of our lives that many Christians use, that phrase to rationalize why they cannot forgive. They will say "I know I should forgive BUT……." Then come the excuses. Do you know what they did to me? I will forgive them when they say they are sorry. I want to forgive them but I just do not feel it in my heart. If I do not forgive them then maybe they will learn a lesson. I will forgive them when I get over the hurt they did to me. None of these excuses can change the command of Jesus to forgive others. We need to be thankful that God does not use any of these excuses when He forgives us of our sin. If we had to earn God's forgiveness, like we feel others have to earn ours, what a mess we would still be trapped in.

A quick look through the Bible will show us that none of these excuses will hold water when we are standing in front of Jesus. Can you imagine looking Him in the eye and telling him that you could not forgive someone because they hurt you too much? One you look at the scars on His hands and I am sure that excuse would be gone. I want you to take time here and look up the following three passages of scripture, Matthew 18:21-35, Colossians 3:12-13, and Mark 11:22-25. These passages make it very clear about our responsibility to forgive others and how this forgiveness relates to God's forgiveness of us. There is no room for options, it is forgive, and God will forgive you. The parable in

Matthew 18 really sums up how a lot of us act in our everyday life. Here Jesus tells us about a servant whose master forgave him a great debt. The servant then goes out and finds someone who owes him a very small amount. At this point you would expect the servant that was forgiven much to forgive the other person. Instead he takes the one that owes him and has him put in jail. God has forgiven us of much yet when someone does the least little thing to us we want to hold it against them. Many times we are that wicked servant.

There are two aspects to forgiveness that I believe we have to address when we are talking about this subject. The first is the ability to forgive ourselves and the second is to forgive others. There are many that may not have an issue with forgiving others while at the same time they cannot and will not forgive themselves for things they may have done. We will take a look at both these issues but first we must look to the Bible and see what forgiveness is and what it is not.

Let us look at what forgiveness is not. The first thing it is not is a warm feeling towards another person. There are some people who think that to forgive another person they must have a certain feeling toward them and it is the presence of that feeling that dictates when they can forgive someone who has wronged them. The reality is when we get that feeling then forgiveness is not really the issue but the issue for people is now how actually to enact that forgiveness. It then just becomes about whether we actually go to that person or if that is even possible. Usually when the feeling comes it just means we have worked through the hurt and enough time has passed that it is not that important to us anymore. It really goes down to the fact that this way of determining when I can forgive someone makes forgiveness about us and our rights not about our responsibilities. It is like the old saying, that time heals all wounds; forgiveness is not about healing your wounds. It is however, about being obedient to the calling that God has put on your life.

Forgiving is not forgetting. You have heard the old saying that we need to forgive and forget and we feel this is Biblical. We have been told that God, when he forgives us, he forgets our sins. This is actually not true. How can God, the one that created the universe, all powerful one, actually forget something? When we forget something it is actually not something we want to do, yet we say when we forgive someone we must forget as well. The reality is when God forgives our sins He does not forget but He chooses to remember them no more. I know that this is a subtle difference but it is a very important one as well. When we forget what someone has one to us it is really not such a great accomplishment on our part. However, when we chose not to remember or can I say when we chose not to bring it up that is something we actively do in our hearts and minds.

Let us take a moment to look at where the notion of God forgetting our sins come from and what the Bible really says about it. I would first say the notion comes from us. We know that if we forget what people do to us then it is easy to forgive them and so we put this human attribute onto God. If we cannot remember what someone has done to us then we will no longer hold them responsible for their actions. We need to look at a couple of passages from the Bible to see where we get this from and look at what they actually say. Take a look at the following two verses.

"For I will forgive their wickedness and will remember their sins no more" (Hebrews 8:12).

"As far as the east is from the west, so far has he removed our transgressions from us" (Psalm 103:12).

As you read these verses I believe you understand where we get the idea that God forgets our sin but we can also see that this is not what they say. Let us take a look at the first verse. In this chapter of Hebrews, it is comparing the old covenant with the new one. This particular section is a quote from the book of Jeremiah. It is talking about a time when God's laws will be written on men's hearts, and of course this time is now. It is talking about a time of restoration, and God is telling the people who when this comes He will forgive them and remember their sins no more. It is important to state here that He does not say he will forget them. Instead the concept is that He will choose not to remember them. It is a conscious decision on His part. He is not saying that He will simply forget about what happened so He will not be able to hold them accountable for them. Instead it is the concept that He will not bring them up to them and hold them accountable for what He has forgiven them for.

As we look at the second verse from Psalm 103 it is important to note hear that I only showed this verse out of the whole chapter for a reason. This is the verse that most people often quote when it comes to how they view God and how He deals without sin. It is from this verse where David writes that God removes our sin as far as the east is from the west and they use this and the previous verse in their mind to tell us that God forgets our sin. A little closer look at this verse in its context will show us that forgetfulness is not what David is talking about. Take a look at the previous verses to this one.

He made known his ways to Moses, his deeds to the people of Israel: The Lord is compassionate and gracious, slow to anger, abounding in love. He will not

always accuse, nor will he harbour his anger forever; he does not treat us as our sins deserve or repay us according to our iniquities. For as high as the heavens are above the earth, so great is his love for those who fear him; as far as the east is from the west, so far has he removed our transgressions from us.(Psalm 103:7-12)

The interesting part of this passage is the notion that God's love is so great for us that He does not treat us as our sins deserve. Again, it is not that He forgets what we have done and therefore He does not punish us for them. It is, however, that He chooses not to hold them to our account and that is because of His great love for us. We see how we are to live this out in our lives in the following scripture from Paul's letter to the Corinthians. *Love is patient, love is kind. It does not envy, it does not boast, it is not proud. It does not dishonour others, it is not self-seeking, it is not easily angered, it keeps no record of wrongs (1 Corinthians 13:4-5).*

It is because of His great love for us that He sent His son Jesus to pay the penalty for those sins. This may seem to you like a small point but the danger of thinking that God actually forgets our sins play out in two harmful ways in us. First, when it comes to forgiving ourselves we know that we generally never forget what we have done so when Satan brings those things to our minds we can be deceived into believing that if we still remember them then God must remember them as well so we think that we either have not been forgiven or we think we have to hold on to them in our own hearts. The fact is that God, once forgiveness has been given is no longer going to hold those things to your account so why should you hold them against yourself. The second way that this can be harmful is the fact that when we forgive others we know deep down we may always have that memory so we may think that if we remember what has happened we have not really forgiven that person. We will look at this again when we look at what forgiveness really means.

There are times when forgiveness really gives us more benefits than it does the one that we have been harbouring a grudge toward. There are many times in our relationships that the person we are upset with the most is not even aware off the fact that they have offended you. Even worse yet they may not care that they have done something that has hurt you. There is the spouse that is upset with the other one, and yes it can work both ways. The one goes up to the other and asks them what is wrong and the answer is "nothing". They expect the other one should be able to figure out what the problem is, especially since it is all about something they have done. The only problem is that the one that offended the other has no idea of what they did to deserve the wrath of their spouse. The question would be who is suffering the most for this unforgiving spirit? I can remember a time in college when I was going into the library and a friend stopped me on the way in to ask for forgiveness. I was completely unaware that there was a problem that existed.

In Hebrews 12:15 it talks about being unforgiving. *"**See to it that no one falls short of the grace of God and that no bitter root grows up to cause trouble and defile many.**"* This verse is placed in a chapter that does what I would call turning the corner. The book of Romans up to that point has outlined the problem we have with sin, and it has given us the solution for that problem. The book spends a large amount of time outlining the theology of salvation. Then Paul starts this portion of the letter with the phrase, therefore. He has laid out the basis for our faith and then he tells us now because of all what I have told you previous this is how we ought to live as Christians. That is what that simple word therefore really means. In the verse previous to this one he talks about living in peace with all and the next verse he talks about being sexually immoral and godless. What could all these thoughts that are strung together have in common?

They all fit together because when we allow an unforgiving attitude to live inside our hearts it will turn into the bitterness that the passage is talking about. When we allow this to live in our hearts it will lead to all manner of sin in our lives because we will never be as close to God as we need to be when we harbour a grudge against someone. This bitterness will filter into every aspect of your life and it can easily overtake you. You will be suffering while others are living the abundant life that Jesus intended for us to live. As a person remains unforgiving they will often try to come up with ways that they may exact revenge on the person they are focusing on when all along God has told us that it is up to Him to get revenge. Why would we want to waste time doing God's job? God is the perfect judge so who better to give out the punishment when it is required. It will consume their lives and they will become unfruitful in their Christian walk.

When we allow this sin to be a part of our lives we are also giving place to the devil to work. We are allowing him to have a foothold in our lives. The reality is that it is him we are listening to not God when we refuse to forgive someone. Would you rather listen to God, the one who wants to give you life abundant or to the thief that has only come to steal and destroy? Most times forgiving someone for a wrong they have done to us will free us more than it will free them. We can see from this that forgiving others will benefit us greatly: However, forgiveness is not something we do just because it is good for us and we will receive a benefit from it.

Although it is true that forgiving others will free us and that it will bring peace to us but that is not why we do it. If we tell people it will be good for them and it will help them move on with their lives then what do we do if they tell us that they do not want to feel better about themselves? In fact if the only reason we forgive others is to feel better and to help ourselves, have we really forgiven? I do not want to minimize the fact that forgiveness is healthy for us it is simply that I do not want us to do it for selfish reasons. We have to forgive regardless of our feelings, as I mentioned earlier, we forgive because God commanded us to forgive and because He has forgiven us.

So what is forgiveness? Simply put forgiveness is releasing another person from a debt that you feel they owe you because of something they have done to you. We could say it is not holding something against another person because of a perceived or an actual wrong they committed toward us. To understand this we need to look at how God forgives us. After all He tells us to forgive because we have been forgiven. *"Bear with each other and forgive one another if any of you has a grievance against someone. Forgive as the Lord forgave you" (Colossians 3:13).*

So how does God forgive us? The first thing we need to look at is the fact that the Bible tells us that while we were still sinners, while we were His enemies Christ died for our sins. He did not wait until we were sorry for what we had done to provide a way to reconcile us to God. The fact is Christ made a way for us when we could do nothing. Note that for those that are reading this book, God made a way to forgive us long before we were even born. He had planned for this before the foundations of the earth. He made a way for us before we even knew that we needed that forgiveness. Romans 5:8 tells us, **"But God demonstrates his own love for us in this: While we were still sinners, Christ died for us."**

The second point we need to remember is the fact that Jesus forgives freely. We do not have to do something to earn His forgiveness. He does not say okay I have made the way of forgiveness, I have done My part. Now here is how you have to earn this forgiveness. Here is the list of seven feats you must complete and then you can come to me and enjoy my forgiveness. Does that concept sound familiar? You cannot go the Bible and find rules that you must follow and then you will be forgiven. In fact when we search the scriptures we will find out that the complete opposite is true. The rules we find in the Bible are about what we do after we have been made into new creations by accepting His forgiveness and making Jesus Lord.

If you take time to study through the book of Romans you will discover the depravity of people. Romans 3:23 tells us, **"For all have sinned and fall short of the glory of God."** You will find out how there is absolutely no way we could ever earn God's forgiveness. The point of Romans is to show you the fact that the only way we can be reconciled to God is through the atoning work of Jesus in His death, burial and resurrection. Here is what Paul tells us, in the Book of **Ephesians 2:8-9, "For it is by grace you have been saved, through faith—and this is not from yourselves, it is the gift of God not by works, so that no one can boast."** So here we are at one point in our lives we are desperate sinners, we have no hope and we are destined to pay the price of sin. That price is death and eternal separation from God. There is nothing we can do to earn forgiveness. But the good news is that even before you realized your sinful condition. Before you realized that there is no hope. Jesus made a way to give you that forgiveness. Before you even realized you needed forgiveness He made a way to get you out of his mess and reconcile you to God and make you into a new creation and made it possible for you to live the type of life that would be pleasing to Him. He did the work to make us into saints.

The third point we will look at is, the fact, that when God forgives us, we are forgiven forever. This forgiveness is not temporary and based on our future actions. I need to mention here that once we are forgiven and we make Jesus lord of our lives there will be a difference in our actions and how we live our lives but this is not the payment to continue in forgiveness it is instead the response to that forgiveness. It is the result of forgiveness not the price. It is in this concept of being forgiven forever, where the notion of forgive and forget, comes in as mentioned earlier. It is not that God forgets but that He does not hold those to our account anymore.

Have you ever been in an argument with someone, or done something to someone, what is the tendency of that person to do? It is to bring up our past wrongs. They bring them up to show you just how bad of a person you really are and how and why it will be difficult to forgive you. This is not how God operates; He forgives and does not hold them against us anymore. When we fail and we ask God for forgiveness this is what it tells us in 1 John 1:9 that God does ***"If we confess our sins, he is faithful and just and will forgive us our sins and purify us from all unrighteousness"***. God does not bring up all the things that we have done before and try to destroy us. When we do ask for forgiveness and our past is brought up that is Satan lying to you about God's grace. Because God has forgiven us in this way this is how we are to forgive others when they wrong us. We are to follow God's example in the way we live our lives.

Questions for Reflection:

1. What excuses have you or are you using not to forgive someone?

2. Has anyone forgiven you when you did not deserve it?

3. When you do not forgive someone do you find yourself harbouring wrong feelings toward them and then acting in ways towards them because of those feelings?

Mark Tollefson

7

The Two Sides of Forgiveness

"Therefore, as God's chosen people, holy and dearly loved, clothe yourselves with compassion, kindness, humility, gentleness and patience. Bear with each other and forgive one another if any of you has a grievance against someone. Forgive as the Lord forgave you."

Colossians 3:12-14

In the previous chapter we took a quick journey through forgiveness. We looked at what it was not and we looked at what it really means to forgive. We as well looked at how God forgives us and the fact that we can do nothing to earn that forgiveness. Now in this chapter we need to take a look at what all this means to us and how it relates to us forgiving those that have wronged us. We will look at two sides of this subject. We will look at our need to forgive ourselves and our need to forgive others.

The first part of forgiveness I want to address is that of forgiving ourselves. There are many Christians walking around that have never been able to bring themselves to forgive themselves for wrongs they have done in their lives. Some of these things were done before they came to Christ and some of them were done after they became Christians. The problem is that when you cannot forgive yourself you are setting up standards for yourself that are higher than God's. You are really saying that you have higher standards than a holy God. You are saying that in a way, you hate sin more than God. What you are really doing is believing in the lies of the Devil. And the Bible tells us that he is a liar and was from the beginning.

"You belong to your father, the devil, and you want to carry out your father's desires. He was a murderer from the beginning, not holding to the truth, for there is no truth in him. When he lies, he speaks his native language, for he is a liar and the father of lies" (John 8:44).

Satan wants you to believe that God has not forgiven you and that there is more for you to do to receive the forgiveness that you crave. He wants you to believe that God could not have possibly forgiven what you have done, after all look at how horrible a sin you have committed. I know there are many people out there that have done what they feel are horrendous things to themselves and to other people. Some of those things weigh on them so heavy that they cannot bring themselves to even verbalize them. God wants you know that He will forgive you, He wants you to know that His Son paid the price in full on the cross. He wants you to know that you do not have to earn that forgiveness, nor could you ever earn such a great gift. He wants you to know you have been redeemed with the blood of His son Jesus.

As Jesus was hanging on the cross paying the price for our sin He verbalizes several sayings. We all have heard many sermons on these sayings but the one I want you think about now is when in the book of John it is recorded that He said "it is finished" and then gave up His spirit. Sometimes we tend to gloss over the importance of this statement and sometimes we seem to think that all He meant was the His life was done but it means so much more than that. When He said it is finished He was saying that the price of sin had been paid. It was a statement that meant there is nothing more to do to pay for our sins, He had done it all. The creator of the universe had just finished paying the price for yours and for my sins. In fact He had just finished paying the price for the sins of the world.

Take a minute right know and just think on that one statement. "It is Finished." Three words that said so much. Jesus Himself told us from the cross that He had completed the task He came to earth to accomplish. He had successfully ransomed us from the penalty of our sins. His death, burial and resurrection had provided the way to reconcile us to God. Do not ever let Satan tell you that you have not been forgiven. Do not let him tell you that you should not forgive yourself or that you are not worth enough to receive the forgiveness that Christ has supplied. There is nothing you could have done that God cannot forgive you for.

Let us take a look at some Old Testament scripture to drive this point home. Take a look at 2 Chronicles 7:14, and what it tells us, *"if my people, who are called by my name, will humble themselves and pray and seek my face and turn from their wicked ways, then I will hear from heaven, and I will forgive their sin and will heal their land."* Here we have God telling the people of Israel that if they humble themselves He will forgive their sins. Now we need to take a quick look at some of the things that they needed to be forgiven for and see if you still think there are some things that you cannot be forgiven for. Here are a few of those sins, they worshiped idols, they sacrificed their children to idols, and they completely disobeyed God, witchcraft, soothsaying, consulted spiritist, and practiced sexual sins to name a few. Yet with all these sins against them we have God promising to forgive them if they seek His face. Do you still think there is something in your life too big for God to forgive?

As we discussed in the previous chapter not only does God forgive us but He promises to remember our sins no more. He told us He will remove our sins as far as the east is from the west. If God will not bring up our transgressions why would we think that there is some reason we should relive them and hold them against ourselves? Sometimes we think we are being very spiritual by hanging on to the wrongs we have committed. Once we have accepted God's forgiveness and made Him lord of our lives we need to realize our identity is in Him. We are no longer sinners we are now saints based on the righteousness of Christ. We must accept the forgiveness He promises to give us and rebuke Satan when he whispers his lies about our guilt. Here again I say, we are redeemed.

Now that we have accepted the forgiveness of the creator of the universe it is now time to obey His command to forgive others. This is not just a suggestion because it would be good for us; it is a command to forgive as we have been forgiven. Maybe we could say it is time to free others as God has freed us. I do realize that some of you are reading this book saying, I would like to forgive but you have no idea what they have done to me. You feel the pain that someone has caused you is just too great to get through. You may have suffered some serious abuse at someone's hands in the past. The fact is that the more suffering you have endured the more critical it is for you to release others.

 Whenever you think too much has happened for you to forgive someone I want you think of Jesus on the cross. He had been falsely accused, He had been beaten, they had ridiculed Him and they had hanged Him on a cross. Look at the following verse carefully. **"Jesus said, 'Father, forgive them, for they do not know what they are doing.' And they divided up his clothes by casting lots" (Luke 23:34).** Notice they wait at the cross for Him to die, where they are casting lots for His clothes, and there is Jesus asking the Father to forgive them because they really do not know what they are doing. Just take a minute to picture that seen in your mind, what a powerful picture of true forgiveness. They are crucifying the Son of God and He forgives them. Is there anything we have gone through that we cannot forgive someone about?

We also need to remember that when we forgive someone it also does not necessarily mean there will be a complete reconciliation with that person. There may be times when you have truly forgiven someone but they have not extended the same forgiveness to you so the relationship will still not be what it should be. Paul addresses this in Romans 12:18, where he tells us, **"If it is possible, as far as it depends on you, live at peace with everyone."** We cannot force others to treat us as they should, all we can do is control our behaviour towards them and I hope they will see the love of Christ in us and change their behaviour so that it comes in line with what God wants from them. Sometimes you will need to forgive someone who has died and obviously you cannot change what that relationship was but you can release them from what it is you think they owe you and by doing this you are in reality releasing yourself. Forgiving someone does not mean the person you have forgiven does not at times have to face justice for their actions. The easy example for this is when a spouse is abusing you. Forgiveness does not mean you would allow it to continue, in fact the best thing you could do after forgiving them is to call the authorities.

There is another misconception out there and people will tell you that in order for you to forgive someone they must first ask for that forgiveness. At one time I would have said the same thing but God has shown me through His word that this is just not the case.

Those that espouse this view will often take Luke 17 and tell us that it is necessary for people to repent in order for us to forgive them but as we look at the context of this passage we will see that this is not what Jesus was really teaching here. When we look at this section we see it is a principle that Jesus is teaching and not a formula. When we see the principle as people must ask for forgiveness we miss the real lesson here. The lesson here was the fact that we are to continuously forgive others no matter how often they offend us. Under the law the Rabbis had said that you only have to forgive someone three times. Now here is Jesus telling people that they must go above and beyond this standard. I believe we could say that He is telling us that we need to be in a constant state of forgiveness. Our lives need to be defined by not only God forgiving us but for our forgiving of others. This is one of those defining character traits of a Christian; it is one of those traits that should set us apart from those that are not Disciples of Christ.

I know some of you may be saying at this point but what about the fact that we have to accept the forgiveness of God before we are forgiven. You may think that again, this shows that before we forgive those, people must repent; however, if we look at what Jesus did we will find that this is just not the case. Romans 5:8 says, **"But God demonstrates his own love for us in this: While we were still sinners, Christ died for us."** The lesson we take from this verse is the fact that Christ provided the way of forgiveness for every one of us long before we ever repented of our sins. He had planned it before the foundations of the earth. He did the work of forgiveness and as we looked at earlier there is nothing we can ever do to earn it and nothing we could ever do to deserve this great forgiveness. When we repent we are not really enabling His forgiveness but we are simply responding to what He has already done. Our repentance was not necessary for Jesus to do what was required to reconcile us to God. He made a way to release us from the penalty of sin, and we just accept it, we do not complete it, He did it all in His death, burial and resurrection.

We need to remember as well that when we forgive those that have offended us we are simply being obedient to our calling. 1 Peter 1:1-2 tells us the following, **"Peter, an apostle of Jesus Christ, To God's elect, exiles scattered throughout the provinces of Pontus, Galatia, Cappadocia, Asia and Bithynia, who have been chosen according to the foreknowledge of God the Father, through the sanctifying work of the Spirit, to be obedient to Jesus Christ and sprinkled with**

his blood: Grace and peace be yours in abundance." So we can see here that this is part of our calling as the elect of God. This is simply not an option it is a requirement of discipleship. When we think that we cannot forgive we need to remember forgiveness is part of our marching orders. When you start a job you are given a job description. This contains all the details of what the company that is hiring you will expect from you as you perform your job. In the same way when we become disciples of Jesus forgiveness is part of our job description.

God also tells us that we need to forgive because we have been forgiven. Sometimes we can forget that we have been forgiven of a lot and it can happen that after we have walked with God for a long period of time that we forget where we have come from. We forget we were every bit as guilty of sin as those that have wronged us. Ephesians 4:31-32 tells us**,** ***"Get rid of all bitterness, rage and anger, brawling and slander, along with every form of malice. Be kind and compassionate to one another, forgiving each other, just as in Christ God forgave you."*** You may think but wait a minute here, I know I have been forgiven but I really did not do anything that bad before I followed Jesus, so I have not really been forgiven of much. You need to re-evaluate that thought again. The Bible tells us that before we came to Christ we were His enemies, we find that in Romans 5:10. Just think about that for a moment, you and I were enemies of the creator of the universe, we were enemies of the one that did more for us than anyone we know now, or will know can ever do for us. An enemy is one that is hostile to the other party, did you ever consider that you were at one time hostile toward God. And He did it while we were still His enemies. You were the same as the soldier that nailed Jesus' hands to the cross; in fact it was your sin, and my sin that made it necessary for that soldier to drive those nails through the creator's hands, and feet. Do you still think that you have not been forgiven of much? Read on.

When we talk about forgiving as God forgave us I want us to think about our Lord on that cross. When He looked down from that cross and said Father forgive them for they know not what they do, I want you to transport yourself back to that moment in your mind and think of what and who He saw from that cross when He prayed that prayer. Looking down He most likely could still see the religious leaders that wanted Him on that cross and that were still hurling insults at Him. He would have seen the soldiers that mocked Him and beat Him. He may have been looking directly at the actual soldiers that drove those nails through his flesh. He could see His mother that I am sure was grieving for

Him. He could see His followers, although there, keeping their distance. And yet with all this fresh in His mind He chose to forgive them. While it was still all in progress He chose to forgive. While they were still taunting Him, while death was not far off, while most people still did not understand, He chose to forgive.

With all that as our backdrop He is our example to follow. We say we want to be like Jesus. We wear the bracelets of what would Jesus do. Do we really? Are we ready to offer, that type of forgiveness? Can we look directly into the face of the one that is offending us and at the same time speak these words; I forgive you as God has forgiven me. Jesus did, and we are told to be imitators of Him, so we must.

We now can talk about the reasons we benefit from forgiving others. We should not just be forgiving people because it is good for us, but the truth is we may receive more benefits from forgiving than those we forgive. We talk about setting others free but the one that we also set free by forgiving is us. In fact in some situations the person that has offended us and we are holding back forgiveness from may not even be aware that we are upset with them. We may be going through our days and holding a grudge and carrying the weight of an unforgiving attitude and the other person is blissfully unaware of our struggle. You may have finally decided to be obedient to your calling and forgive and maybe it is a time when you go up to them and express that forgiveness and they are very surprised that there was a problem in the first place. It turned out that you had been the one actually paying the price for not forgiving all this time. Just think of the time and energy you spent holding that grudge and trying to get what you thought you deserved from that person.

Part of forgiveness is the realization that it is not up to us to exact revenge on those that have hurt us, it knows that it is not our responsibility nor is it our right to even up the score. Too often we say we cannot forgive because we are working through you feelings when the real problem is that you will not forgive until you get your revenge. Do we not know that it is God's job to judge and to punish? Or do we just want to forget about that so that we can do what we feel is right in our own eyes. I know that we sometimes feel it is our right to get revenge on our enemies but the truth is when we come to the cross we give up our rights and our only goal should be to bring glory to God. We need to die to our selfish needs and be more concerned about furthering God's kingdom instead of our own. Sometimes it will require us to allow our hurts to go unanswered and leave it to God's justice. Romans 12:19 tell us, **"Do not take revenge, my dear friends, but leave room for**

God's wrath, for it is written: "It is mine to avenge; I will repay," says the Lord."

If you think that you just cannot forgive. If you are sitting there reading this book and you are troubled because you want to follow God's command to forgive but you just do not know how to accomplish this. It is not that you are making excuses but you truly want to fulfill what God has for you. I want you to remember the words of Paul, found *in* **Philippians 4:13, "I can do all this through him who gives me strength."** As we look at this statement, I am aware that this is one of those verses that are often times taken out of context. We use it to encourage us when we want to do something we think would be good for us. But if we look at the context here, we will get the real meaning behind it and it will hold more meaning and be much more encouraging. We need to remember here that Paul wrote the book while sitting in a prison. The verses preceding these talk about how Paul has learned how to be content in all his circumstances. He has learned to live with little and with plenty. The key to this living is doing it all through Christ that strengthens. We can live out the calling of God because of Jesus and what He did for us. So as you do all to follow the commands of God do it with the help of God, we cannot live the life God has intended for us, by ourselves or on our own power. We can only live it through the power of the Holy Spirit.

Questions for Reflection?

1. As you honestly examine yourself are there things in your life that you do not think that God could ever forgive you for?

2. Do you really understand that it is Satan that wants you to believe that lie?

3. As you reflect why have you at times not forgiven someone, what excuses did you use?

Mark Tollefson

8

The ME Generation

"The Son is the image of the invisible God, the firstborn over all creation. For in him all things were created: things in heaven and on earth, visible and invisible, whether thrones or powers or rulers or authorities; all things have been created through him and for him."

Colossians 1:15-16

There was a time in our history and it was not all that long ago that man thought that the sun and other planets actually orbited around the earth. You definitely could say we really did think we were the centre of the universe. It was not until a few hundred years ago that we realized that it was the other way around. We discovered that we were not the centre of the universe and in fact the earth revolved around the sun. This may seem to you to be a crazy theory and you may wonder how anyone could believe such a thing. To understand how anyone could come up with such a hypothesis you only need to understand from what point they were looking at the world. If you do a little research you can find out that man came up with this thought by observing the sun and the stars and the visible planets from our vantage point here on earth. They were looking at the universe from their limited vantage point. If that was all we were able to do today was go outside and look from our perspective we would have come up with the same theory.

The fact of the matter is that whenever we look at any situation from our own perspective only, we will always come to the conclusion that it is really all about us. Once we start looking outside our own interests the picture will change drastically. The interesting result of our awareness that the earth revolves around the sun instead of the sun revolving around us is the fact that it had what I would consider to be the opposite affect that one would expect. I would have thought the once we realized that we were not the centre of the universe we would begin to feel a little smaller and set our priorities to the correct order. But that is certainly not what happened. Now we are even more self-centred than we have ever been. Whereas before the modern era we realized how little we knew. Now we are so proud because we think we are able to figure everything out. What has happened is that the more we know the smarter we think we are as a people? We have become proud of the fact that we can figure so much out on our own, or so we think. Now more than ever we really do think that everything is about us.

So here we are today living as Christians in a world that tells us that we need to get all we can and that the only thing that matters to us is making ourselves happy. We have been trained to just accept the fact that self comes first. We just need to look around at the world we live in to see how much this thinking has pervaded society. Take a look at the advertising on television or radio or on your Facebook account. On Facebook and other online sites they actually tailor the advertising to you specifically and item they feel you would be interested in buying. Everywhere we look the marketers are telling us that if we just buy this product or that one we will be happier. When was the last time you were sold a product which will make you a better servant?

If you have a satellite radio you know that there is a station for every kind of taste. If you are listening to something you do not like all you have to do is change the channel until you find something that appeals to you. We are even taught this when it comes to our relationships, including our marriages. If I am friends with you and you do something I do not like I just find another friend and with modern technology I can just block you, whether it be on my phone, on Facebook or anywhere else. All a sudden in my mind you do not exist. In marriage I am told that if it does not work out I just leave and find someone else that is more to my liking, after all the world tells me that the only reason to marry is to make me happy. We are told that life is all about us. The individual is all that matters. We are inundated with writings and speeches about the importance of the individual. We rarely will hear anyone tell us that it is more important to be concerned about other people and you will never hear that we should actually put others before ourselves.

If we get offended we are told to file a complaint and the offender will be dealt with. If we are accused of something it is always someone's or something else's fault. We live in a society where there is no such thing as personal responsibility, unless we feel someone other than us should be responsible for their actions. If there is something we want we are told to obtain it by any number of means. If we do not have enough money we are told to just get another credit card. If someone else has something we feel we are entitled to then we want someone to take it off them and give it to us. We live in a culture of entitlement. The world tells us that there is no reason we should not have something we think will make us happy. We are at a point where personal debt is at an all-time high, partially because we are told that we are all entitled to the finer things in life which will bring us enjoyment. If my neighbour has something then I am entitled to it as well. How many parents are tormented because they cannot afford to buy their kids brand name clothing? After all we are told that our children need that to find complete happiness.

So here we are living in a world that is trying to sell us one ideal and the God of creation telling us that the complete opposite is true. God tells us that if we truly want a satisfying life, a life that actually glorifies our Father in heaven then we need to deny ourselves. John puts it simply for us *in **John 3:30, "He must become greater; I must become less."*** These words were spoken by John the Baptist when his disciples were distressed because Jesus was baptizing people and some people had said that there are more people going to Jesus. John responds to them realizing that it was to be about Jesus and not about him. It was not a competition among John and Jesus. What John was doing was actually all about Jesus. How often do we get caught up in the same type of feelings that John's disciples were experiencing? How many times do you see a ministry or a church promoting themselves almost more than they are promoting the Good news of the Gospel? When we have the attitude that John the Baptist had, the attitude that God wants us to embrace we are going against the culture of today.

Unfortunately, instead of rejecting the world's thinking, we have taken the worlds teaching on the importance of self, and have accepted it in the church. We can see it in different manifestations. We see people in churches today where the only thing that matters to them about the service is how it affects them. Some have lost the idea of a church service challenging them and instead are looking to be entertained. We see people going from one to church to another until they find one that appeals to them. The church becomes more about meeting their own needs than it does about equipping them for service. Some churches will even cater to this glorification of self by offering services that appeal to certain people as opposed to services which will glorify God.

We are told that to minister to others we need to feel well about ourselves. They tell us that if it is inconvenient for us to serve than we just say no.

Ministering to others becomes about what is easy for us to do and what will not interfere with our schedule instead of what God is calling us to do. In some circles, we are even told to interpret scripture based on what works for us. Then we hear all those buts again. I know the word is being preached here but I am bored, the service is too long. I know I should work in Sunday school but it would be hard for me to show up on time. I know I should be reading my Bible more but I have more important things to do. On it goes; people will have all sorts of excuses why they should not inconvenience themselves to do the things they really know God has for them. They have bought into the world's thinking that if something is not comfortable for me, or if it requires something of me that I do not enjoy, surely God would not want me to do it. Can you imagine how the world would take notice if we would just reject this worship of the self and follow Jesus?

The other side of the coin is a type of self-denial more than dying to self. Many people will not do certain things because they think it will make them more spiritual. They think that if they are suffering in some way then that is what Jesus meant when He asks us to pick up our cross and follow Him. It is really the same form of legalism that the Pharisees practiced in Jesus' time on earth. It becomes a way of self-promotion instead of dying to self because people who practice this really want people to notice them and how much they have given up for God. It can become a source of pride for them.

Jesus addresses this in **Matthew 6:5-6 and 16-18.** *"And when you pray, do not be like the hypocrites, for they love to pray standing in the synagogues and on the street corners to be seen by others. Truly I tell you, they have received their reward in full. But when you pray, go into your room, close the door and pray to your Father, who is unseen. Then your Father, who sees what is done in secret, will reward you." " When you fast, do not look somber as the hypocrites do, for they disfigure their faces to show others they are fasting. Truly I tell you, they have received their reward in full. But when you fast, put oil on your head and wash your face, so that it will not be obvious to others that you are fasting, but only to your Father, who is unseen; and your Father, who sees what is done in secret, will reward you."* People that fall into this category equate dying to self with creating a certain amount of personal discomfort. The interesting thing to note about these people is that even they will have their limits on this type of self-denial. There are still certain things they will not give up.

So what does it mean when scripture tells us to pick up our cross, what does it mean to die to self? Simply put it is the process of denying the flesh attitude of only thinking about ourselves. It is about giving up our rights and completely submitting to the will of God. It is submitting to God's ways even when our flesh side tells us that it seems unfair to us personally. It is realizing the only thing that really matters in this life is bringing God glory. It is the acceptance that God is the one that we need to base our life on, He does not exist to serve us.

A good passage of scripture that drives this point home is found in Colossians. ***"For in him all things were created: things in heaven and on earth, visible and invisible, whether thrones or powers or rulers or authorities; all things have been created through him and for him. He is before all things, and in him all things hold together. And he is the head of the body, the church; he is the beginning and the firstborn from among the dead, so that in everything he might have the supremacy" (Colossians 1:16-18).***

Does this sound like a God that is there to serve us? It is interesting that Paul tells us that He created all things and they were created for Him. How many times have you been told that the earth was created for you? This passage tells us the opposite. It reminds us everything is about bringing glory to God not to us. Take a minute here and read Romans 1:20 and Psalm 19. Do these passages make you think that it is all about you or God?

There are some that would say if all this was made for God and His glory then in fact I am insignificant and where is my self-worth. Your self-esteem comes from knowing where you fit into this whole plan of God's. Remember He has made us a big part of His plan for this world. In fact He has chosen to use us to reach the world for Him. If you stop and think about that for a minute you will realize what and incredible honour it is to have the creator of the universe to decide to let us become part of His plan. Our self-esteem or our self-worth comes from knowing our place in God's grand scheme. Listen to the words of Jesus in John 15:1-17 *"You are my friends if you do what I command. I no longer call you servants, because a servant does not know his master's business. Instead, I have called you friends, for everything that I learned from my Father I have made known to you. You did not choose me, but I chose you and appointed you so that you might go and bear fruit—fruit that will last—and so that whatever you ask in my name the Father will give you. This is my command: Love each other".*

Can you just imagine that the creator of everything. The one that created it all and the one whom it was created for calls us friends. And more than that He tells us that He has told us what He has learned from the Father. He chose us. We would think it a great thing if some person on earth that we held in high regard called us their friend. If the leader of a country was to get up in front of the news crews and let the world know that you were their friend that would make most of us feel pretty good about ourselves. While, the king of all kings, the creator, the Lamb of God, the one that was before all things and in whom all things are held together has let the world know that you are His friend. Do you really need anything else to boast your self-worth? How could you not die to self and completely submit to God. I cannot overstate the fact that the creator of the universe knows my name, speaks to me through His word, paid the price for my sin and has made me part of His great and wonderful plan. I think the word incredible does not even come close to expressing the magnitude of this truth.

The obvious example of how to live a life where we die to self and give up our will to His would be the life of Jesus. Let us take a look at His life to see how we ought to live ours. We can start by looking at the incarnation. Read what Philippians 2:5-11 says about this subject and just meditate on it for a moment *"In your relationships with one another, have the same mindset as Christ Jesus: Who, being in very nature God, did not consider equality with God something to be used to his own advantage; rather, he made himself nothing by taking the very nature of a servant, being made in human likeness. And being found in appearance as a man, he humbled himself by becoming obedient to death— even death on a cross! Therefore God exalted him to the highest place and gave him the name that is above every name, that at the name of Jesus every knee should bow, in heaven and on earth and under the earth, and every tongue acknowledge that Jesus Christ is Lord, to the glory of God the Father."*

We see here Jesus becoming one of us, experiencing the life we live and all of its limitations. The passage talks about Him emptying Himself and taking on the role of a servant. The passage tells us that He had every right to claim equality with God but He gave up His rights for us. He emptied Himself for us. How many kings do you know that would give up their rights to benefit you? Since Jesus is to be our example to follow why is it that we think our rights outweigh the rights of those around us and even are more important than God. This may sound like a drastic to statement to make but fact is that every time we use the word BUT when it comes to a Biblical truth or command that is really what we are saying. When we accept one of God's instructions and then do not follow it because we come up with a reason that we either have a better way or that there is an exception to it for you that is what we are doing. We are saying our rights trump the Bible. We are not following Jesus' example of giving up what we feel are our rights. We need to remember here that Jesus actually did give up the rights He actually did have, whereas we only think we have them when in fact it is God that is the one that is allowed to determine those rights. We look to the world to see what our privileges and rights are and the Bible is telling us to look to God.

Let us continue to look at Jesus' life as our example. As we read through the Gospel we are struck with the fact that everything Jesus did while here on earth was about the Kingdom. We can also say the only goal that mattered to Him was doing the will of the Father. John 6:38 tell us, **"For I have come down from heaven not to do my will but to do the will of him who sent me"**. From the start of His time here to the Ascension that was all that mattered to Him.

We can even see this at the age of 12. It is recorded in the Gospel of Luke in chapter 2 the story of His family's trip to Jerusalem. On the way back home after a day's journey they discover that Jesus is not with them. His parents go back to look for Him and find Him after three days in the temple talking the priests. When His mother questions Him about what He has been doing Jesus tells her **"Why were you searching for me?" he asked. "Didn't you know I had to be in my Father's house?" (Luke 2:49).** Even at that age He is focused on His mission. How many 12 year olds do you know with that kind of focus?

When we look at the short time of what we consider his ministry years we see that everything He did was about showing the way of the kingdom and reconciling man to God. He is not at all concerned about what kind of house He has or how many cattle He has acquired or how big a car He can get. He did not go around worrying whether someone is going to get something He did not have. Jesus was not concerned with keeping up with the Jones. In fact, in Luke 9 He tells some people that want to follow Him that even foxes have holes but the Son of Man does not even have a place to lay His head. This is certainly not the message some want to hear today. A person cannot get anymore counter culture with an attitude like that. We actually think that we are entitled to all the blessings that God has given to us. Unlike the world's thinking, we do not have the right to any of this, but in God's infinite grace, He provides these comforts for us. Everywhere Jesus went His concern was for others, for us.

When He was going to Jerusalem for the last time and He is fully aware of what is about to happen and He takes time to weep over the city and its people. *"And when he drew near and saw the city, he wept over it, saying, "Would that you, even you, had known on this day the things that make for peace! But now they are hidden from your eyes. For the days will come upon you, when your enemies will set up a barricade around you and surround you and hem you in on every side and tear you down to the ground, you and your children within you. And they will not leave one stone upon another in you, because you did not know the time of your visitation"* (Luke 19:41-44).

They are about to beat Him, mock Him and crucify Him yet He is more concerned for them than He is for Himself. That is truly dying to self. What an example for us to follow. Do you think that if you were in that position you would have the same attitude that Jesus did at that time in His life?

Then we get to the garden and His prayer. Here we have Jesus at the lowest point in one respect but at the same time He is at the culmination of His earthly journey. Jesus is in the garden praying and was in such agony Luke tells us His sweat was like blood. He is telling His father how He is feeling. He is pouring His heart out to the Father. He asks God that if it is possible, if there is some other way to accomplish this, that is what He would like. But then He says not my will but your will be done. He recognizes that there is more to His mission than just His feelings.

Is there a better example of dying to self? Everything He had done up to this point had been for others, everything had been about the fulfillment of His mission. And now it is still not about Him but it was all about redeeming His creation, it was about reconciling us to God. He knew that He had to give up His rights and that He would not be in comfort but He still choose that it would be about us not Him. There is no greater example of giving up our own rights; after all they crucified Him for crimes He did not commit. It is important to mention here that Jesus willing gave up His life; they did not take it from Him.

So how did Jesus give up His rights and only focus on others throughout His time on earth? I believe there are three things that He did to accomplish this goal. I need to say here that some would say that the reason that He could accomplish this was because He was God. When we say this, it in some peoples mind, excuses us when we do not measure up to this standard. But remember the Bible clearly teaches that He was completely man and at the same time was still God. I want you to know that we can live up to the standards He has set for us. And that we should live up to that standard. That should be our goal.

The first part of what Jesus did to accomplish this was to have an eternal outlook. If we could only keep our eyes on eternity it would change the way we live our lives in the here and now. The problem we encounter with this is that as soon as we take our eyes off eternity we begin to think that all that matters is this life. The minute that this life becomes the focus we will not be able to die to self because we will want to get everything we can out of this life. When we realize that our span on this earth is very short compared to the eternity that we will spend with our Lord, our focus will have to be different. We will realize that the short time we spend here dying to self to accomplish God's purpose will pale in comparison to the eternity we will spend in the joy of the Lord and being in His presence. When we get this eternal perspective we will gladly give up our rights and our will to have Christ live through us and by doing this it will bring others into the kingdom so they can share in the joy of the Lord for eternity.

There are many people who have spent time just surviving in the hopes that they can make their lives better on this earth. Some may sacrifice many things to attend a college in the hopes of a better job for the time they are on this earth. When we see them do this we will respect that sacrifice. How much more should we sacrifice for the sake of eternity. If 4-8 years of hard times to go to school is deemed to be an acceptable sacrifice to gain maybe 50 years or so of ease. Is it not worth giving up your will to God for an eternity of life with our Saviour?

The second part of what Jesus did was that He knew and kept His mind on the end. What was the result of His mission? As we said it was the forgiveness of sin and our reconciliation to God. He knew that He had to suffer for a short time but He knew what that suffering would accomplish. So what is our result of our dying to self? Well it is to bring others to God. We are to put others first so that they can see the love of God in us. We need to live this life in a way which will attract people to the Gospel. Like Jesus, we need to be the gospel message in flesh and bone. Everything we do needs to be with that result in mind. As Jesus' only concern was to do the Father's will to reconcile people to God that needs to be our only concern, nothing else matters. How big a house we have, what kind of job we have, what kind of car we drive, how much we have in the bank. None of that matters; it is all about bringing people to the cross. 2 Corinthians 5:18 tells us **"All this is from God, who through Christ reconciled us to himself and gave us the ministry of reconciliation"**. This is what are result needs to be. This is the mission that was given to us by God Himself. This mission is what gives meaning to our lives. If we spend a lifetime of collecting stuff and treasures here on earth and then we die and leave all that behind, what have we really accomplished? But, when we spend our lives keeping our eye on the mission He has given us to do, when we die there will be eternal rewards that we cannot even imagine.

The third part of what Jesus did was to keep His focus always. He never lost focus as we sometimes tend to do. A while ago I was watching Nik Wallenda cross Niagara Falls on a tight rope. The one thing I was fascinated by was the amount of focus he had on the task at hand. Not for a moment did he lose sight of his goal. It was interesting to watch him at the end of his crossing, when he knew he had made it, he ran into the arms of his family. It was a great picture of us, at the end of our earthly existence we will run into the arms of our Saviour. If Nik had have lost his focus there could have been dire consequences for him.

In the same way, can you imagine if Jesus had lost His focus and forgot what He came to do. Where would we all be now? Our focus needs to be kept on Jesus and His mission. We do not want to get caught up in the pursuits of the pleasures of this world because all this will do is to break our focus. I remember when I was being taught to drive a car my driving instructor would tell me not to look straight down in front of the car but to look down the road at the big picture. If I got distracted and only looked directly in front of my car I would lose touch with what I was driving into ahead of me. That could have spelled disaster. In the same way when I concentrate on this life and my own rights and what I want for me and forget about the bigger picture of God's plan it could spell disaster for me and those around me.

In 1 Corinthians 9 Paul talks about his rights. He tells the church that he had a right to be supported by them. He tells them he did not have to work, it was reasonable for him simply expect to be supported. But he goes on to tell them that although it was a right for him he gladly gave up that right. And why did he do that? He tells us in 1 Corinthians 9:12 the following, **"If others have this right of support from you, shouldn't we have it all the more? But we did not use this right. On the contrary, we put up with anything rather than hinder the gospel."**

There you have it, Paul dying to self, giving up what really were his rights and all for the sake of the gospel. May we all that are Christians catch this vision and live out our calling. May we give up everything for the sake of the Gospel of Jesus Christ. Our lives cannot be about us, our lives must be about furthering the Kingdom of God. We need to realize that there is a world out there that is on the wrong road. A road that leads to destruction. We need to be willing to give up all to rescue the perishing. When we keep our eyes set on this mission the things of this world just so seem so unimportant anymore.

Last year in October my mother went into the hospital where she stayed until her death this year. News year's day was a difficult one for her. She was more confused than ever. At about 5:30 that evening she had a seizure and went into a coma and she never regained consciousness. The following day while I was visiting her I could not help but notice the fact that the nurses had neatly piled what belongings she had with her in the corner of her hospital room. At that moment I was reminded of what everything we spend our lifetimes acquiring really amounted up to. At the end of our lives our belongings will be piled up somewhere and they will be disposed of in some way. They will at that moment, no matter how important they seemed to you, be of no consequence. As I stood there taking in this scene I was overwhelmed with the knowledge that the only thing that mattered at that moment was what she had done with and for Jesus. Thankfully my mother had been reconciled to God through Jesus so it really did not matter what happened to the stuff she had acquired. She had won the biggest prize there is, an eternity with God.

Question for Reflection

1. Are there areas of your life that you are holding back from God and trying to use them to satisfy yourself?

2. What areas of your life are keeping you from focusing on the mission that God has given us?

3. Who really comes first in your life, you or others, be honest?

4. What are you not willing to give up for God?

There Are No Buts Except The One You Are Sitting On

9

The Beginning

"Everyone who competes in the games goes into strict training. They do it to get a crown that will not last, but we do it to get a crown that will last forever."

1 Corinthians 9:25

As you come to the end of this book there is one conclusion I do not want you to reach. I do not want you to look at the chapters in here and get discouraged. I do not want you to think that you somehow do not measure up to God's standard now so there is no use in even trying.

We need to remember, as we look back on the truths I have shared with you that we are all at different places in our journey with God. We are not all at the same level of maturity in our walk with the Savior. In 1 Corinthians 9, Paul, uses the analogy of a race to talk about our Christian life. When we think of a race, we need to remember some things. Not everybody is in first place, or even, second place. We all have a spot in the race but they will all vary. The point, Paul made, was that we do not have to be in first place, but to finish the race. If we look at marathon races, and that really is what this life is, we will see there will be a lot of runners, and all will finish with different times.

What one needs to remember is that no matter where you are in the race, you are still better off than the person sitting in the stands watching the race. Even if that person has the best seats right at the finish line, they are still not in the race, and they will never finish. If the person that was sitting in the stand decides that at the end they want to walk across the finish line, it really does not mean much, because they have never started the race. We need to look at ourselves and make sure we are in the race.

There could be a temptation when you are in last place in such a race to give up but that is not what I would want for you today. When you are behind a bunch of runners it may seem that it is really no use to carry on. After all you do not have the strength to compete with the other better runners. This is where Jesus comes into the picture. As you take time to look at where you are in the race my hope would be that it would inspire you to train harder and gain the few places from where you are now. Living this life as a disciple of Jesus is a lifelong endeavour.

As we commit ourselves to Him, we start a process which will continue to shape us into the people who the Lord wants us to be. What I wish for you, is for you to allow God to continue the work that He has begun in you. I want you to look at your life and see where you do not measure up to God's standard and then ask that He will bring you to the place where you need to be to bring glory to Him. My hope for you as you went through this book would be that you would have experienced one of the following two responses. You may have read this book and thought that you agreed and that is how you are living you life and although we can always improve you are on the right track. The second response may have been on of conviction. You may have realized that there are areas of your life that you have been ignoring the commands of scripture. If that is you then please do not let it end there make sure you bring the way you live your life with the way God tells us to in His Word.

In 2 Corinthians Paul is addressing the Corinthian church for the second time. If you read the words written so long ago, they not only sum up the heart of Paul, but they express my heart, as well, and what I want in turn for you taking the time to read this book. *"Even if I caused you sorrow by my letter, I do not regret it. Though I did regret it—I see that my letter hurt you, but only for a little while— yet now I am happy, not because you were made sorry, but because your sorrow led you to repentance. For you became sorrowful as God intended and so were not harmed in any way by us. Godly sorrow brings repentance that leads to salvation and leaves no regret, but worldly sorrow brings death. See what this godly sorrow has produced in you: what earnestness, what eagerness to clear yourselves, what indignation, what alarm, what longing, what concern, what readiness to see justice done. At every point you have proved yourselves to be innocent in this matter. So even though I wrote to you, it was neither on account of the one who did the wrong nor on account of the injured party, but rather that before God you could see for yourselves how devoted to us you are. By all this we are encouraged"* (2 Corinthians 7:9-13).

In a lot of churches today they try to avoid causing anyone to sorrow in their shortcomings. As we see in this passage when that godly sorrow brings repentance it is not something to be avoided, it is something we should all be happy to experience. When we look at our lives and see where we are not living out our calling we need to be brought to a place of true repentance. We need to start to take the steps necessary to bring our lives into line with what God has for us and stop making excuses of why it is impossible to live the life that the Bible teaches us about.

You will have noticed as you went through this book, that most of the issues we talked about revolve around the question: how much of my life will I to give to God? Am I really able to die to my own selfish animations? I know for some people the thought of giving it all to God is a scary proposition. I know that there are people who have thrown their complete and absolute trust in another person and they have been greatly hurt by that same person. You may feel because of that you cannot give up your all to anyone or even to God.

Some will think that if they just keep a little back for themselves than they will somehow still be in control and then they will be able to achieve happiness and success. It is with that in mind that I want to leave you with some encouragement. Read the words of

Deuteronomy 31:8 *"The Lord himself goes before you and will be with you; he will never leave you nor forsake you. Do not be afraid; do not be discouraged".*

If we can only get our heads around how much God really loves us and how He really wants the best for us it would be a lot easier to submit totally to Him. People may and will at times let you down but God will never fail you, you can fully trust Him with everything. I want to assure you here that there is no greater fulfillment than that of completely abandoning your own will and plans to the plans of God. Any plans we have that we think will bring us happiness pale in comparison to the absolute thrill and contentment when you know that the God of the universe is using you to complete His work here on earth.

Last year during the Christmas season my mother spent several weeks in the hospital. One day while I was Christmas shopping with my granddaughter, Kira, I decided I would take her in for a short visit with her great-grandmother. Before we went into the hospital I had told Kira how the hospital had some large inflatable Santa's and several decorated Christmas trees. As we went inside I showed her the Santa above the front entrance door and the Christmas trees in the lobby. She seemed to be more impressed with the large inflatable Santa over the front door.

From the windows on the floor my mother was on you could see onto one roof. From one window in particular you could see an inflatable Santa riding a John Deere tractor. You need to know that the day before we went to visit with Mom the area had experienced a snow storm and there were high winds with that storm. As we got to the floor mom was on I took Kira to the window to see Santa on the tractor. As you may imagine when we got to the window we discovered that the storm on the previous day had blown Santa over and deflated him. Kira thought it was very funny and the first thing she did when we saw my mom was to take her to the window to see what had happened to Santa.

This takes me back to the passage I quoted from Matthew in the first chapter of this book. When Jesus talks about what happens when we build a house on sand and what happens when we build a house on the rock that is Jesus. Like that Santa on his tractor was blown over after the storm we will be blown over if we continue to allow the world's way of doing things to come into the church and mix the world's philosophy with God's word. This is what happens to our lives when we continuously use the word *BUT* to rationalize why we do not need to follow the instructions that God has given us in His word. When we build our lives on a foundation of *BUTS* we will find that not only will life be less than the abundant life that Jesus intended for us, we will also find that it is very difficult to live it out without coming to ruin. We will find that our lives will be somewhat deflated just like that Santa on the tractor. Those that are around us that do not know God yet will see us in our deflated state and will not be attracted to the God we serve. How much glory is brought to God when we are out of air? There may be a little air left in us but we will miss so many of the blessings that God wants to give us.

This is not just the end of a book it is a beginning. We can go now and live out this life in the power of the Holy Spirit and by doing that draw others to Jesus. May our lives never be about us. May the one purpose of our lives be bringing glory to God.

Questions for Reflection

1. The obvious question here is in what ways are you not living up to biblical standards?

2. What will you commit to do to change the way you are living and interacting with others?

3. Will you commit to allowing the Spirit of God work in you so that you will glorify Him in all you do?

Mark Tollefson

ABOUT THE AUTHOR

Mark Tollefson is and elder in his local church and has spent years teaching Sunday school and various Bible studies. Mark has four children and three grandchildren. His passion is to help people grow in their walk with God so that they can enjoy the abundant life that Jesus came to give us.

Mark Tollefson

www.ingramcontent.com/pod-product-compliance
Lightning Source LLC
Chambersburg PA
CBHW022359040426
42450CB00005B/251